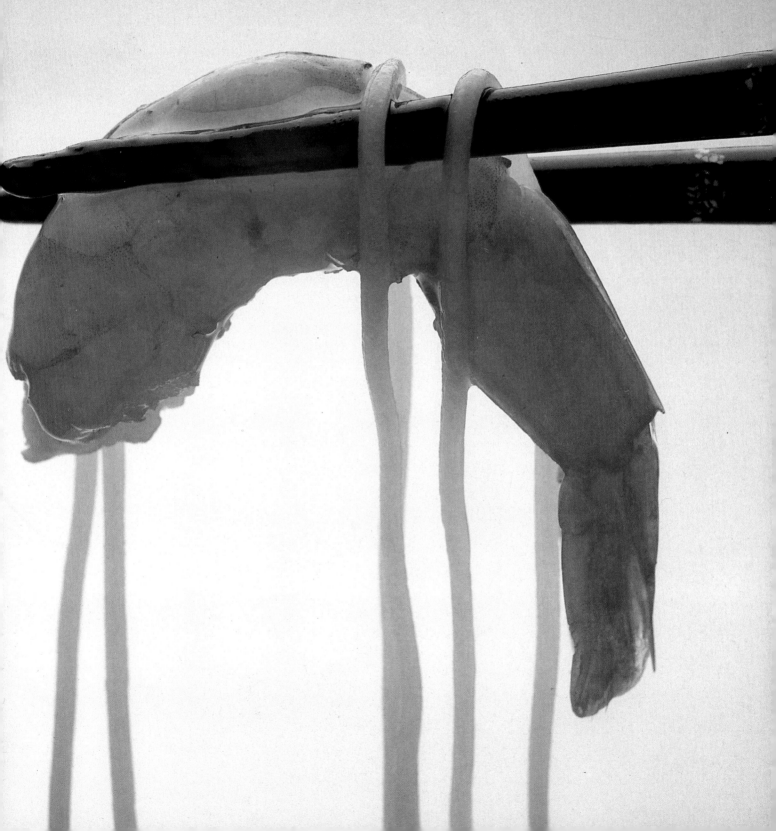

This edition first published in 1993 by
Sunburst Books, Deacon House, 65 Old Church Street,
London, SW3 5BS

Copyright © Editorial LIBSA, Narciso Serra, 25 – Tel 433 54 07 –
28007 MADRID
4.ª EDICION 1991
Copyright English language text © 1993 Sunburst Books

ISBN 1 85778 007 8

Printed and bound in China

CHINESE
AND
JAPANESE COOKING

CONTENTS

INTRODUCTION
Chinese Cuisine

The immense land mass of China, with its diverse climates and broad range of geographical, ethnic, cultural and social conditions, offers a cuisine which incorporates many different styles and tastes. The Chinese cuisine is difficult to classify, but it can be divided into five basic groups:
1. The so-called Imperial cuisine of Peking and Shantung in the north eastern region. This is a subtle and sophisticated style of cooking with delicately spiced dishes.
2. The cuisine of the western region of Sze-Tchuan, characterized by simple stews, which are always very spicy.
3. Also inland, but further east, is the region of Ho-Nan, where the famous sweet and sour dishes are prepared using numerous different spices.
4. On the continental shore of the Formosa Channel is the region of Fu-Cheu, famous for its fish and seafood dishes, and, above all, for its delicious soups, which it is customary to serve at the end of the meal in China.
5. Finally there is the Cantonese cuisine and its much more europeanized derivative from Hong Kong. This is the best known Chinese cuisine in the West due to the large number of Chinese immigrants from Hong Kong. Fried foods are predominant and delicate seasoning is used. This is the cuisine most palatable to western tastes.

One of the outstanding characteristics of Chinese cookery is the great variety of products used in food preparation. This might give the impression of an excessive love of luxury which drives chefs to search for the rarest and most sophisticated products for their dishes. However the truth is that the Chinese cook aims to take advantage of all available ingredients.

Most Chinese cooking methods are the same as those used in the West; namely boiling, braising, frying, steaming and roasting. But the most common technique consists of stir-frying the ingredients for a very brief time over a high heat with a small quantity of seed-based oil. This is undertaken in a special pan with a rounded base, called a "wok." The method of stir-frying originally evolved from a desire to save fuel. All the ingredients for stir-frying are cut into very small pieces, so that their cooking time rarely exceeds five minutes. This means a great deal of preparation beforehand. Seasonings must be measured and all ingredients ready to cook, since any delay can jeopardise the final result.

When preparing a dish for stir-frying, the cooking time of each individual ingredient should be considered, so they can be added to the wok in the right order to ensure that each one is perfectly cooked.This process will become automatic with practice.

This type of cooking precludes any prior preparation or freezing of ingredients, since the consistency and texture of the ingredients is very important. Vegetables should remain crunchy, and fish and meat should be prepared and cooked in such a way that they retain all their juices.

The staple food of the Chinese people is rice, rather than bread. But in the northern region its use is more limited and it is often substituted by wheat or other grains, especially millet. These are refined into flour-like forms and used as the basis for accompaniments to the main dishes.

Unlike the traditional style of meal in the West, there is no main course in Chinese cookery, as all the courses are endowed with equal importance. At a celebration or formal meal a series of dishes is served. According to an ancient ritual, this series begins with four cold dishes, which will have been placed on the table beforehand. This is followed by another four dishes, or a multiple of four. It is traditional that, at formal meals, there will be four dishes or a multiple of four for each serving, although this rule does not apply to informal family meals. The second serving usually consists of fried or sautéed food. When this is served to the host's table, he must give a toast with the words "Kan Pei" (Your good health), at which the guests express their appreciation for the invitation. Afterwards other roast or steamed dishes are served accompanied by rice or an alternative type of grain product. Finally according to Chinese custom, the meal ends with one or two soups. Desserts do not exist, as sweet dishes are served indiscriminately with the others. Between servings it is customary to rest, drink, chat or play various games. When a meal is served without ceremony all the dishes are placed on the table at the same time. Thus the host can join the guests once the meal has been served.

The Chinese table is round and dishes are usually laid out to form a square with the soup tureen in the centre. Nothing on the table has a purely decorative function, although the array of crockery is usually very colourful at a Chinese table. Each setting consists of a bowl for rice, another bowl for soup, a flat plate for the solid food, a small dish for the sauces and seasoning, a small deep bowl for the sweet dishes, a cup for wine or tea, a small porcelain spoon for the soup and a pair of chopsticks. As all the ingredients are chopped into bite-size pieces in the kitchen, there is no need for knives at the table.

Chinese wine, usually made from rice, enhances the taste of dishes. The most popular is Sho Hsing. There is a custom whereby some bottles are buried on the day of a child's birth and then consumed at their wedding celebration.

Chinese of all social classes drink tea, especially in Peking, where there is little rain and the relentless Mongolian wind causes dehydration. It is considered a sign of welcome to offer a cup of tea to visitors on any occasion. This offering of tea is an ancient ritual which has survived since Imperial times. It is oneof the most prized traditions in China, especially as it enables the hosts to display the beauty of their china.

The tea is prepared by placing a small spoonful of tea leaves in a china cup with a lid. Boiling water is poured over the leaves; this is then covered and left for three minutes, after which the tea is ready to be drunk. To drink it, the lid is lifted to one side and the tea drunk through the opening, avoiding the leaves which remain inside the cup. The Chinese don't add milk or sugar to the infusion as is common in the West.

Note: The ingredients mentioned in this book are common throughout the Far East – on the islands as well as the mainland. However many are also well known and can be acquired without difficulty in the West. The more exotic ingredients are usually found only in special shops or in Chinese and Japanese restaurants. If it is possible to substitute more accessible, less exotic ingredients, then this is stated in the recipe. As a general rule, sherry, brandy or cognac can replace Chinese rice wine or Japanese sake.

Table of Measures:

$\frac{1}{4}$ cup: 60 ml or $\frac{1}{16}$ litre
$\frac{1}{2}$ cup: 125 ml or $\frac{1}{8}$ litre
1 cup: 250 ml or $\frac{1}{4}$ litre
2 cups: 500 ml or $\frac{1}{2}$ litre
3 cups: 750 ml or $\frac{3}{4}$ litre
4 cups: 1,000 ml or 1 litre
1 tablespoon: 20 ml or 4 teaspoons
1 teaspoon: 5 ml
1 glass: 200 ml or $\frac{1}{5}$ litre

Top: Chinese Chicken Stock (recipe on page 12)
Bottom: Chicken with Clams (recipe on page 8)

POULTRY

SMOKED CHICKEN

Serves 4

1 x 1 kg/2.2 lb chicken
1 tsp salt
1 tsp peppercorns
3 tbsp brown sugar
2 tsp sesame seed oil

Boil the whole chicken for 40 minutes. Drain and rub the inside and outside with a mixture of the salt and peppercorns, coarsely crushed with a rolling pin.

Place 2 tablespoons of the sugar in a large saucepan. Place the chicken on a grill or round cake rack inside. Cover the saucepan and seal the lid with aluminium foil to prevent any steam escaping.

Cook gently for 10 minutes to smoke the chicken with the vapour from the sugar. Discard the burnt sugar, replace with the remaining sugar and repeat the process for a further 5 minutes.

Remove the chicken and brush with the sesame seed oil. Finally, slice the chicken and serve hot or cold.

Note: The chicken can also be smoked with pine needles instead of sugar. To protect the saucepan, line with aluminium foil before putting the sugar or pine needles inside.

CHICKEN WITH CLAMS

Serves 4

1 tsp five-spice powder
1 tsp salt
4 tsp cornflour
500 g/1¹/₂lb boneless chicken breasts, diced
2 tbsp oil
1 garlic clove, peeled and crushed
100 ml/4 fl oz chicken stock
2 tbsp cold water
1 medium can clams, drained

Mix together the five-spice powder, salt and half the cornflour. Toss the chicken pieces in the mixture until well coated.

Heat the oil in a wok for a few seconds. Add the chicken pieces and garlic and stir-fry over a high heat for 2-3 minutes until the chicken is golden. Push the chicken to one side of the wok and pour on the chicken stock and the remaining cornflour

dissolved in the water. Stir continuously over medium heat until the sauce thickens.

Stir in the clams, reheat and serve with white rice.

DUCK WITH CHESTNUTS

Serves 6

125g/4 oz dried chestnuts
2 garlic cloves, peeled and crushed
1 tsp grated ginger root
1 tbsp chinese rice wine or dry sherry
1 tbsp light soy sauce
1 x 2 kg/4¹/₂ lb duck
100 ml/4 fl oz peanut oil
3 tbsp red tofu (naam yu)
2 tsp sugar

Place the chestnuts in a bowl and cover with boiling water. leave to soak for 30 minutes, drain and soak for another 30 minutes. Drain well. Mix together the garlic, ginger, wine and soy sauce and rub all over the duck, inside and outside.

Brown the duck in hot oil in a wok, turning several times. Remove the duck and pour away most of the oil. Mash the tofu with the sugar. Return the duck to the wok and add enough water to half cover. Add the chestnuts and bring to the boil. Cover and simmer gently for 1¹/₄ - 1¹/₂ hours until the duck is tender. While cooking turn the duck over occasionally and, if necessary, add a little boiling water if it becomes too dry.

Serve the whole duck surrounded by the chestnut sauce, or cut into pieces first then pour over the sauce. Garnish with cooked baby onions if desired.

FRIED CHICKEN WITH CRAB SAUCE

Serves 4

1 x 1 kg/2.2 lb chicken
1 tsp salt
2 tsp five-spice powder
3 tbsp cornflour
2 tbsp cold water
oil for frying

Crab sauce:
2 tbsp peanut oil
¹/₂ tsp grated ginger root

6 spring onions, sliced
175 ml/6 fl oz chicken stock
125 g/4 oz crab meat
1 egg white, lightly beaten
2¹/₂ tbsp cornflour
1 tbsp cold water
freshly ground black pepper

Cut the chicken into small pieces, rub with a mixture of the salt and five-spice powder and set aside for 30 minutes. Meanwhile, prepare the crab sauce. Heat the oil in a small saucepan. Fry the ginger and sliced onions for 1 minute. Add the chicken stock and bring to the boil. Stir in the crab meat, season with a little pepper and bring back to the boil. Add the beaten egg white, stirring well with a fork. Dissolve the conflour in the water, add to the pan and simmer until thickened, stirring constantly. Keep warm over a low heat.

Mix the cornflour and water to a thick paste and coat the chicken pieces. Drain. Heat the oil in a wok and fry the chicken pieces, a few at a time, over high heat until golden and tender. Drain on kitchen paper towels then serve with the hot sauce poured over.

Top: Duck with Chestnuts
Bottom: Fried Duck with Crab Sauce

CHICKEN IN PINEAPPLE SAUCE

Serves 4

1 x 1 kg/2.2 lb chicken, quartered
oil for frying
1 small onion, peeled and finely sliced
5 slices ginger root, chopped
1 tbsp chinese rice wine
3 tbsp soy sauce
1 tsp salt
1 level tbsp sugar
80 ml/3½ fl oz pineapple juice
80 ml/3½ fl oz cooking juices from the chicken
1 tbsp cornflour
3 pineapple rings, chopped

Fry the chicken quarters in oil until golden. Place in a flameproof casserole dish with the sliced onion, ginger, wine, soy sauce, salt and sugar. Cover and cook over gentle heat for at least 40 minutes until the chicken is tender.

Remove the chicken from the pan, drain and reserve the cooking juices. Remove the flesh from the bones and cut into 5 cm/2 inch lengths. Arrange on a serving dish and keep warm. Place the pineapple juice in a saucepan with the strained cooking juices, cornflour and pineapple pieces. Mix well together and simmer until thickened. Pour over the chicken and serve hot.

STUFFED TURKEY

Serves 6 - 8

1 x 1½-2 kg/3-4½ lb turkey

Stuffing
250 g/8 oz cooked ham
250 g/80 oz calves liver
25 g/1 oz diced bamboo shoots
25 g/1 oz celery, diced
25 g/1 oz cooked chestnuts, diced
2 tsp ginger juice
2 tbsp soy sauce
1 tsp sugar

Sauce:
2 tbsp soy sauce
2 tbsp sesame seed oil
1 garlic clove, peeled and crushed
1 tbsp ginger juice
1 tbsp cornflour
salt

Rub the turkey outside and inside with salt, wash with hot water and dry with a tea towel.

Combine all the stuffing ingredients and stuff the turkey. Truss to secure the stuffing. Rub the turkey with oil and salt, place in a roasting dish and roast in the oven at 180°C/350°F/gas mark 4, allowing 30 minutes per ½ kg/1 lb. Increase the oven temperature for the last hour of roasting.

Meanwhile combine all the sauce ingredients and bring to the boil.

Place the cooked turkey on a serving dish, after removing the trussing. Coat with the sauce and serve very hot. The flesh of the turkey should be very tender so that it can be handled easily with chopsticks.

Opposite: Chicken in Pineapple Sauce
Below: Stuffed Turkey

CHINESE CHICKEN STOCK

1 chicken carcass
1¹/₂ litres/2¹/₂ pints water
6 peppercorns
2 celery sticks with leaves, roughly chopped
1 onion, peeled and quartered
few springs of fresh coriander
2 slices ginger root
salt

Place the chicken carcass in a saucepan, add the water and the remaining ingredients and bring to the boil. Cover and cook for 45 minutes to 1 hour. Strain and leave to cool. When cold, remove any traces of fat by drawing a piece of kitchen paper over the surface of the stock.

This stock can be used as a basis for soups and sauces.

CHICKEN WITH GINGER AND LOTUS BUDS

Serves 4

25 dried lotus buds
1 x 1 kg/2 lb chicken
6 peppercorns
2 tbsp peanut oil
1 garlic clove, peeled and crushed
pinch of salt
1 heaped tbsp chopped fresh ginger
75 ml/3 fl oz Chinese rice wine or dry sherry
1 tbsp honey
50 ml/2 fl oz light soy sauce
1 star anise

Chop the chicken into small pieces.

Soak the lotus buds in hot water for 20 minutes, drain, remove the stalks and cut each flower into 2 or 3 pieces. Dry roast the black peppercorns in a saucepan and crush in a mortar.

Heat the oil in a wok, add the garlic, salt and ginger and fry over gentle heat until golden. Add the chicken pieces and fry over a moderate heat until browned.

Add the drained lotus buds, pepper, wine, honey, soy sauce and star anise. Cover and cook gently for 25 minutes. If necessary, add a little water at the end of the cooking time.

DUCK WITH BAMBOO SHOOTS

Serves 4

1 x 1 kg/2.2 lb duck, boned
1 tsp cornflour
1 tsp water
100 g/4 oz broccoli, chopped

1 tbsp oil
6 slices ginger root, chopped
1 garlic clove, peeled and chopped
100g/4 oz bamboo shoots, finely sliced
¹/₂ tsp salt
1 tsp sugar
¹/₂ tsp freshly ground black pepper
5 tbsp chicken stock
1 tsp Chinese rice wine or dry sherry
¹/₂ tsp sesame oil

Chop the duck into small pieces and place in a shallow dish. Mix together half the cornflour and water, pour over the duck pieces and leave to marinate for 20 minutes. Cook the broccoli in boiling water for 1 minute and drain thoroughly.

Heat the oil in a wok and fry the ginger, garlic and bamboo shoots for 2-3 minutes, stirring continuously. Add the salt, sugar, pepper, stock, wine and sesame oil, and stir for 3 minutes. Add the remaining cornflour dissolved in the water and stir continuously until the sauce is thick.

CHICKEN FOO YUNG

Serves 2

125g/4 oz boneless chicken breasts
3 tbsp water
1 tbsp Chinese rice wine
¹/₂ tsp salt
1 tbsp cornflour
6 egg whites
10 tbsp sesame oil

Sauce:
2 tbsp oil
8 small bamboo shoots
8 mange-touts or 2 tbsp peas
150 ml/¹/₄ pint chicken stock
1 tsp salt
1 tbsp cornflour
3 tbsp water

Chop the chicken breast into small pieces. Place in a mixing bowl and add the water, a little at a time, mixing thoroughly. Add the wine, salt and cornflour, and mix well.

- Beat the egg whites until stiff and add to the chicken mixture. Heat the oil in a wok and pour in the mixture. Remove from the heat immediately and stir briskly, then return to heat. Cook until the mixture is set, but unchanged in colour.

To make the sauce, heat the oil in a saucepan. Fry the bamboo shoots and mange-touts, and whie they are still crisp add the chicken stock and bring to the boil. Combine the water, salt and cornflour, and stir into the sauce.

Place the chicken on a serving dish, pour over the sauce and serve hot.

Top: Chicken Foo Yung
Bottom: Duck with Bamboo Shoots

SEAFOOD

HO NAN MULLET

700g/1¹/₂ lb grey mullet (or other whole white fish), scaled and cleaned
2 tsp salt
8 small onions, peeled
1 grated ginger root
2 tbsp peanut oil
2 tsp sesame seed oil
2 tbsp light soy sauce

Remove and discard the head and tail of the mullet. Boil enough water to cover the fish in a wok. Add the salt and the mullet, cover and cook gently for 5-7 minutes, then drain. Fry the onions and ginger in the peanut oil, add the sesame seed oil and soy sauce, and stir well.

Place the fish on a cooked lettuce leaf and serve immediately covered in the sauce.

Below, top: Fish Stock
Below, bottom: Ho Nan Mullet
Opposite, top: Fish Dumplings
Opposite, bottom: Fried Fish (recipe on page 16)

FISH STOCK

Makes 1.7 litres/3 pints

fish heads and bones, prawn heads and other scraps
2 litres/3¹/₄ pints cold water
10 peppercorns
3 slices ginger root
1 carrot, peeled and quartered
2 celery sticks, roughly chopped
1 large onion, peeled and quartered
2 sprigs coriander

Wash the fish and prawn scraps, place in a large saucepan and cover with the cold water. Add the remaining ingredients and bring to the boil. Cover and cook for at least 1 hour. Strain and use as stock in fish soups or other seafood dishes.

FISH DUMPLINGS

Serves 2

250g 8 oz white fish fillets
1 tbsp ginger juice
¹/₂ tsp salt
4 slices ham, cut into strips
few leaves of spinach, cut into strips

Dumpling batter:
100g/ 4 oz flour
1 egg
100 ml/4 fl oz water
1 tbsp sesame seeds

Cut the fish fillets into pieces 10 cm x 4 cm (4 in x 1 ¹/₂ in). Rub with the ginger juice and salt and set aside.

Mix together the ham and spinach to make the filling. Put a little mixture onto each fish piece, roll the fish around the filling, and fix in place with a toothpick.

Combine all the dumpling batter ingredients, adding the sesame seeds last of all. Dip the fish rolls in the batter and fry in very hot oil. Serve immediately.

FRIED FISH

Serves 2

250 g/8 oz white fish fillets
2 tbsp Chinese rice wine or dry sherry
1/2 tsp salt
pinch of cayenne pepper
2 tbsp cornflour
1 egg white
oil for frying

Cut the fish fillets into oblong pieces about 4 cm x 2 cm (1½ in x ¾ in). Sprinkle with the wine, then with the salt and cayenne peper, and finally with a tablespoon of the cornflour.

Beat the egg white with the remaining conflour to make a mixture that is thick, but not too dry. Coat each piece of fish in the batter, and fry briefly in very hot oil. Do not overcook, the batter should remain ivory coloured.

Serve hot on small individual plates with salt and pepper.

STUFFED FISH

Serves 4

1 kg/2.2 lb sea bream (or other whole white fish), cleaned
6 tbsp sesame seed oil

Stuffing:
125 g/4 oz lean pork, chopped
2 tbsp chopped spring onions
1 tsp fresh grated ginger
2 tbsp cornflour
1 tbsp Chinese rice wine or dry sherry
1 tsp sugar
1 tbsp soy sauce

Sauce:
1 tbsp sugar
3 tbsp soy sauce
5 slices ginger root, chopped
1 baby onion, peeled and chopped
1 garlic clove, peeled and chopped
50 g/2 oz capers

Make three cuts on each side of the fish. Combine all the ingredients for the stuffing, and use to stuff the fish.

Heat the sesame oil in a wok and fry the fish until golden on both sides. Combine the sauce ingredients except the capers and add to the fish. Pour over enough water to just cover the fish. Bring to the boil, cover and cook over a moderate heat for 25 minutes. Turn over the fish and cook for another 10 minutes. Serve hot garnished with the capers.

SMOKED FISH

Serves 4

500g/1 lb fish fillets eg sole

Marinade:
4 tbsp white wine or dry sherry
150 ml/¼ pint soy sauce
5 slices ginger root, chopped
2 tbsp chopped onion
1 garlic clove
pinch of black pepper
2 star anise

1 tsp black pepper (optional)

Sauce:
3 tbsp Chinese rice wine or dry sherry
3 tbsp soy sauce
2 tbsp sugar
2 tbsp sesame seed oil
3 tbsp brown sugar
oil for frying (optional)

Use one or more types of fish fillet for this receipe. Cut the fish into 2.5 cm/1 inch strips. Place in a shallow dish and pour over the marinade. Leave to marinate for

at least 3 hours. Remove from the marinade and smoke for 20 minutes (see receipe for Smoked Chicken on page 8).

Meanwhile, place all the sauce ingredients in a pan and bring to the boil.

When the fish has cooled little, cut each slice into 3 and, one at a time, dip them in the sauce. Serve hot or cold.

This dish can be prepared in advance since it will keep for 3 - 4 days.

Note: Instead of being smoked, the fish may also be fried in very hot oil for 15 minutes, using the same marinade and sauce.

JADE AND CORAL PRAWNS

Serves 4

16 large prawns
1 broccoli head
$1/2$ tsp grated ginger root
1 tbsp peanut oil
$1/4$ tsp salt
4 tbsp water
1 tbsp Chinese rice wine or dry sherry
$1^{1}/2$ tbsp cornflour
1 tbsp cold water
1 tbsp sliced preserved red ginger

Remove the shells from the middle part of the prawns, keeping the heads and tails. Make a slit in the belly of each prawn with the point of a very sharp knife.

Divide the broccoli into small florets with a few centimetres of stalk attached. If the florets are very big, cut them in two lengthways. Place the end of each stalk in the slit made in each prawn.

Stir-fry the ginger, prawns and broccoli for 2 minutes in very hot oil. Sprinkle with the salt, water and wine, cover and cook very gently for 3 minutes.

Push the prawns to one side of the wok, add the cornflour diluted in the water and stir until the sauce is thick.

Opposite: Smoked Fish
Above: Stuffed fish

Garnish with red ginger and serve at once with white rice.

FRIED CRAB WITH BLACK BEAN SAUCE

Serves 4

1 cooked crab
1 tbsp salted soya beans, rinsed
1 tbsp light soy sauce
1 tsp sugar
2 garlic cloves, peeled
4 tbsp peanut oil
2 slices ginger root, chopped
175 ml/6fl oz hot water
2 tbsp cornflour
1 tbsp cold water
3 spring onions, peeled and chopped
1 egg, lightly beaten

Remove the crab meat from the body of the shell. Discard the shell, except for the claws. Crack the claws so the sauce can penetrate the shell.

Purée the soya beans and mix with the soy sauce, sugar and one of the garlic cloves, crushed. Heat the oil in a wok and fry the remaining garlic, halved, with the ginger. Remove them and stir-fry the crab for 4-5 minutes over a very high heat. Remove the crab and fry the soya bean mixture for 1 minute, then add the hot water and crab.

Mix everything together, cover and cook for 3 minutes. Add the cornflour, diluted in the water, and stir until the sauce is thick. Finally, add the chopped onions and beaten egg. Stir until the egg has set. Serve at once with white rice to offset the salty sauce.

Note: Salted soya beans are available in cans from Chinese supermarkets.

SCALLOPS WITH RADISHES

Serves 4

8 scallops in shells
16 radishes, peeled and thickly sliced
3 tbsp oil
1 tbsp Chinese rice wine or dry sherry
1/2 tsp salt
100 ml/4 fl oz fish stock
1 tsp cornflour
1 tbsp cold water

Cut the scallops into bite-size pieces. Leave the centres whole.

Heat the oil in a wok, add the radishes and fry briefly. Add the scallops and their juices, then add the stock, wine and salt. Cover and simmer for about 5 minutes or until the scallops are tender. Add the cornflour disolved in the water and the MSG (if using). Mix well and serve hot.

Top: Jade and Coral Prawns
Bottom: Fried Crab with Black Bean Sauce

PRAWNS WITH PINEAPPLE AND CASHEW NUTS

Serves 4

3 tbsp sesame seed oil
50 g/2 oz cashew nuts
2 spring onions, peeled and sliced
25 g/1 oz green beans, roughly chopped
50 g/2 oz cabbage, shredded
50 g/2 oz bamboo shoots, sliced
500 g/1 lb shelled prawns
1/2 litre/3/4 pint fish stock
4 pineapple rings, diced
1/2 tsp salt
1/2 tsp freshly ground black pepper
2 tsp cornflour
1 tbsp cold water

Heat 1 tablespoon of the oil in a wok and stir-fry the cashew nuts until golden. Remove and reserve.

   Heat the remaining oil in the wok and fry the onions for 1 minute. Add the chopped green beans, cabbage and bamboo shoots and continue stir-frying for 2-3 minutes. Add the cashew nuts, prawns, stock, diced pineapple and salt and pepper and continue cooking until the sauce thickens. Serve hot, garnished with whole prawns if desired.

Top: Scallops with Radishes
Bottom: Prawns with Pineapple and Cashew Nuts

PORK AND BEEF

HONEY ROASTED PORK

Serves 4

500 g/1 lb pork fillet
6 tbsp soy sauce
1 spring onion, peeled and chopped
4 slices ginger root, chopped
4 tbsp Chinese rice wine or dry sherry
1 garlic clove
1 tbsp oil
1 tsp sugar
1 tbsp honey

Cut the pork into 5 cm/2 inch strips. Mix together the soy sauce, chopped onion, ginger, wine and garlic and marinade the pork in this mixture for 12 hours.

Grease an ovenproof dish with the oil. Drain the pork from the marinade, brush with a mixture of the sugar and honey and bake in the oven at 200°C/400°F/gas mark 6 for about 35 minutes, turning the pieces once.

Leave to coool then cut into smaller pieces and serve cold.

The pork may be fried, instead of baked. If desired, the honey can be left out.

FRIED BEEF WITH CELERY

Serves 2

250 g/8 oz beef fillet or rump steak
1 tsp cornflour
3¹/₂ tbsp soy sauce
500 g/1 lb celery

Cut the beef into strips. Mix together the cornflour with 2 teaspoons of soy sauce and coat the beef strips in this mixture. Cut the celery into matchsticks, boil for 10 minutes then drain.

Heat the oil in a wok, add the beef strips and fry quickly until brown, then add the celery and the remaining soy sauce. Serve hot.

BEEF WITH LOTUS ROOT

Serves 4

250 g/8 oz beef fillet
1 tbsp light soy sauce
¹/₂ tsp salt
1 garlic clove, peeled and crushed
¹/₂ tsp grated ginger root
¹/₄ tsp five spice powder
2 tbsp peanut oil
100 ml/4 fl oz beef stock
1 tbsp cornflour
2 tbsp cold water
12 slices preserved lotus root

Cut the meat into paper thin slices. Combine the soy sauce, salt, garlic, ginger and five spice powder, pour over the meat slices and mix well.

Heat the oil in a wok and stir-fry the meat over a high heat until brown. Add the stock and the cornflour dissoved in the water, bring to the boil and cook, stirring continuously until the sauce thickens. Add the lotus root, reheat and serve with white rice.

STIR-FRIED BEEF WITH PEAS

Serves 6

500g/1 lb fillet of beef
2 tbsp light soy sauce
¹/₂ tsp salt
6 dried mushrooms
250g/8 oz peas
3 tbsp oil
4 spring onions, peeled and chopped
1 tbsp Chinese rice wine or dry sherry
¹/₂ tbsp sugar
100 ml/4 fl oz beef stock
3 tsp cornflour
1 tbsp cold water

Cut the meat into thin slices and marinate in the soy sauce and salt for 30 minutes. Soak the mushrooms in hot water for 30 minutes, remove the stalks and thinly slice the heads. Blanch the peas in boiling salted water for 2 minutes. Stir-fry the meat in 2 tablespoons of the oil over high heat until browned. Remove and reserve. Clean the wok, heat the remaining oil and stir-fry the mushrooms and onions for 1 minute.

Add the wine, sugar and stock, and bring to the boil. Add the cornflour dissolved in the water, and cook, stirring continuously, until the sauce thickens.

Add the meat and peas to the wok, stir again and serve at once with white rice.

Top: Fried Beef with Celery
Bottom: Stir-fried Beef with Peas

GOLD COINS OF PORK

Serves 4

500 g/1 lb pork fillet
80 g/3½ oz pork fat
10 dried mushrooms
oil for frying

Marinade:
4 tbsp soy sauce
2 tsp Chinese rice wine or dry sherry
1 tsp grated ginger root
½ spring onion, peeled and chopped
2 star anise

Sauce:
2 tbsp sugar
½ tbsp sesame seed oil

Cut the pork fillet and pork fat into small round slices about 1 cm/½ inch thick.

Soak the dried mushrooms in hot water for 30 minutes then remove the stalks. Combine all the ingredients for the marinade, add the pork fillet, pork fat and mushrooms, and marinate for at least 1 hour. Remove the pork and mushrooms, but reserve the marinade.

Using strong skewers, which are square-sectioned if possible, make kebabs by alternating pieces of meat, fat and mushrooms. Deep-fry the kebabs very quickly. Meanwhile, heat the marinade in a pan and add the sauce ingredients.

Take the pork, fat and mushrooms off the skewers and serve very hot, garnished with baby corn, if desired. Serve the sauce separately.

Square sectioned skewers are recommended, because the square hole in the centre of the cooked rounds of pork makes them look like ancient Chinese golden coins.

PORK CHOP SUEY WITH EGGS

Serves 4

5 dried mushrooms
14 tbsp oil
250 g/8 oz pork fillet in one piece
250 g/8 oz spring onions, peeled and sliced
125 g/4 oz bamboo shoots
250 g/8 oz bean sprouts
25 g/1 oz fresh noodles
3 eggs
¼ tsp salt

Seasoning:
½ tsp salt
1 tbsp Chinese rice wine or dry sherry
2 tbsp soy sauce

Soak the dried mushrooms in hot water for 30 minutes. Drain and remove the

stalks. Heat 5 tablespoons of the oil and fry the pork and onions together. Cut the meat into strips. Fry the vegetables and the noodles in 5 tablespoons of the oil. Mix together in a deep bowl the pork strips, the vegetables and noodles and add the seasonings.

Lightly beat the eggs with the salt, and fry them in 4 tablespoons of the oil to make an omelette, stirring to cook evenly but ensuring that the omelette stays intact.

Finally place the omelette on the chop suey and serve hot.

Take care not to overcook the onions and bean sprouts or they will lose their flavour.

Opposite: Gold Coins of Pork Below: Pork Chop Suey with Eggs

BEEF STOCK

Makes about 1.4 litres/2½ pints

1 kg/2.2 lb beef bones
500 g/1 lb stewing beef
1.7 litres/3 pints cold water
1 onion, peeled and quartered
1 stick celery with leaves, roughly chopped
1 star anise
4 sprigs coriander or parsley
3 tsp salt

Place the bones and meat in a large saucepan and add the other ingredients.

Bring to the boil, cover and simmer for at least 2 hours. Strain and allow to cool then chill in the refrigerator. When the stock is cold, skim the grease off the top.

Use in soups and sauces for meat dishes.

PORK WITH FIVE FLOWERS

Serves 6

1 kg/2.2 lb lean pork, diced
4 tbsp thick soy sauce
2 tbsp Chinese rice wine or dry sherry
1/2 tsp five spice powder
1 garlic clove, peeled and crushed
75 g/3 oz long grain rice

Marinate the pork in a mixture of the soy sauce, wine, five spice powder and garlic. The longer the pork is left to marinate, the better it will taste.

Dry roast the rice for 15 minutes in a frying pan, stirring continuously. Then grind the grains to powder.

Drain the diced pork from the marinade and roll in the rice powder, coating well. Place in a steamer and steam for 2 hours. The meat should be tender enough to separate with chopsticks. Garnish with paprika, if desired, and serve hot with white rice.

STUFFED CHINESE CABBAGE LEAVES

Serves 5

10 leaves Chinese cabbage

Stuffing:
125 g/4 oz lean beef or pork, finely chopped
3 tbsp finely chopped onion
1/2 tsp salt
1 tsp soy sauce
1 tsp cornflour

Sauce:
1 tsp soy sauce
1 tbsp wine vinegar
2 tbsp sugar
2 tsp cornflour
3 tbsp cold water

Blanch the Chinese cabbage leaves, drain and cut into 13 cm x 5 cm/5 in x 2 in lengths. Keep the leftover scraps.

Mix together all the ingredients, and divide the mixture into 10 portions. Place one portion of stuffing on each leaf, folding the leaf around the stuffing and pressing down lightly.

Line the sides and base of a steamer with the leftover pieces of Chinese cabbage, arrange the stuffed leaves on top and steam for 15 minutes or until cooked through. Arrange on a serving dish.

Place the soy sauce, vinegar and sugar in a pan and bring to the boil. Add the cornflour dissolved in the cold water and 50 ml/2 fl oz of cooking liquid from steaming the stuffed leaves. Bring back to the boil and pour over the stuffed cabbage. Serve hot.

PORK STOCK

Makes about 1.4 litres/2½ pints

500 g/1 lb pork bones
1.7 litres/3 pints cold water
3 slices ginger root
1/4 tsp peppercorns
2 baby onions, peeled and halved
1 stick celery with leaves, roughly chopped
1 carrot, quartered
4 small sprigs coriander or parsley
1 tbsp light soy sauce
3 tsp salt

Place the pork bones in a large saucepan and cover with the water. Bring to the boil slowly, stirring frequently. Add the spices, vegetables and herbs and cook for at least 2 hours. Season with the salt and soy sauce.

Strain and leave to cool, then chill in the refrigerator. Skim off the grease from the surface and use as directed.

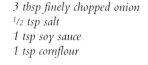

Top: Stuffed Chinese Cabbage Leaves
Bottom: Pork with Five Flowers

PORK AND BEEF RISSOLES

Serves 6

75 g/3 oz shortgrain rice
6 dried mushrooms
250g/8 oz beef fillet, chopped
250 g/8 oz pork fillet, chopped
3 spring onions, peeled and finely chopped
1/2 tsp grated ginger root
1 garlic clove, peeled and crushed
2 tsp salt
1 egg
25 g/1 oz dried water chestnuts, chopped

Soak the rice in cold water for at least 2 hours. Drain and leave to dry on a tea towel while preparing the rissoles.

Soak the dried mushrooms for 30 minutes in hot water (if dried mushrooms are unavailable, fresh mushrooms can be substituted and do not require soaking). Carefully dry the mushrooms, remove the stalks and finely slice the caps.

Place the remaining ingredients in a large bowl and mix well with the hands. Form the mixture into 2.5 cm/1 inch balls. Roll the balls in the rice, pressing down lightly so that the grains stick to the surface.

Line a steamer with greaseproof paper and arrange the rissoles on top, leaving enough space between them for each one to expand. Steam for 30-35 minutes. If the water evaporates too quickly, add more boiling water.

As the rissoles are cooking, the rice will swell to leave them covered with lovely pearls of rice.

Top: Pork Stock
Bottom: Pork and Beef Rissoles

SWEET AND SOUR PORK

Serves 4

500 g / 1 lb pork fillet

A:
1 tbsp Chinese rice wine or dry shery
2 tbsp soy sauce
2 tbsp flour
1 tbsp conflour
oil for frying

B:
3 small green peppers, quartered
1 onion, peeled and quartered
1 carrot, peeled and finely sliced
1 bamboo shoot, sliced
2 pineapple rings, chopped
5 tbsp oil

C:
6 tbsp sugar
4 tbsp soy sauce
1 tbsp Chinese rice wine or dry sherry
2 tbsp wine vinegar
4 tbsp fresh tomato sauce
1 tbsp cornflour

Cut the meat into 4 cm/1½ inch cubes, and mix with all the *A* ingredients except for the oil.

Deep-fry the meat in very hot oil until it is golden and crisp. Drain and keep warm.

Heat 5 tablespoons of oil in a wok and stir-fry the remaining *B* ingredients. Combine all the *C* ingredients, except for the cornflour, and pour over the vegetables. Bring to the boil, and add the cornflour dissolved in 100 ml/4 fl oz water, stirring continuously.

Add the fried pork, mix well and serve hot.

BOILED CHANG CHUN PORK

Serves 3

300 g/10 oz cooked pork
1 tbsp Chinese rice wine or dry sherry
1 tbsp soy sauce
1 tsp sugar
3 tbsp oil
1 large green pepper, halved, deseeded and chopped
pinch of salt
3 garlic cloves, peeled and finely chopped
1 tsp ginger root, chopped
3 baby onions, peeled and sliced in thick rings
1 tbsp hot black bean sauce
1 tbsp hoi sin sauce

Finely slice the meat without removing the fat. It is easier to cut the meat if it has been chilled first. Mix with the wine, soy sauce and sugar.

Heat the oil in a wok, add the chopped green pepper and salt and stirfry over a high heat. When the pieces of pepper are shiny with oil and bright green, remove from the wok.

Pour away all but 1 tablespoon oil, the fry the meat for 1 minute over a moderate heat. Add the garlic and ginger, and continue browning the meat. Add the onions, peppers, wine, soy sauce and remaining 2 sauces, mix well and reheat. Serve hot with white rice.

Opposite: Sweet and Sour Pork
Left: Boiled Chang Chun Pork

EGGS

EGGS COOKED IN TEA

Serves 5

10 eggs
3 tbsp black China tea
2 tbsp salt
1 tbsp freshly ground black pepper
5 star anise
2 tbsp soy sauce

Boil the eggs for 10 minutes, drain and place in a bowl of cold water. When cool, tap the eggs lightly with the back of a spoon to crack the shells, taking care that they don't break completely; the thin membrane beneath the shell should be unbroken.

Boil the eggs with the tea and the remaining ingredients for 20 minutes.

Allow to cool and carefully remove the shells - the eggs will be imprinted with an attractive, marbled effect from the cracks.

EGG FOO YUNG

Serves 6

2 dried mushrooms
250 g/8 oz cooked crab meat, chopped
1 tsp grated ginger root
1 tbsp Chinese rice wine or dry sherry
1¹/2 tsp salt
6 eggs, lightly beaten
9 tbsp oil
6 bamboo shoots, sliced
1 spring onion, peeled and finely sliced
2 tbsp soy sauce
2 tbsp peas
1 tbsp cornflour
1 tbsp water

Soak the dried mushrooms in hot water for 10 minutes. Drain and slice thinly.

Meanwhile combine the crab meat, grated ginger, wine and salt with the beaten eggs. Heat 7 tablespoons of the oil in a 25 cm/10 inch omelette pan or wok and make 1 large or several small omelettes, frying on both sides.

Heat the remaining oil in a pan and stirfry the mushrooms, bamboo shoots and onion. Add the soy sauce, peas and stock. When the sauce boils, thicken it with the cornflour dissolved in the water. Pour the sauce onto the omelette and serve hot.

SCRAMBLED EGG YOLKS WITH BAMBOO SHOOTS

Serves 6

6 egg yolks
225 ml/8 fl oz cold chicken stock
3 tbsp chopped ham
3 tbsp chopped bamboo shoots
1 tbsp Chinese rice wine or dry sherry
1 tsp salt
2 tsp cornflour
2 tbsp cold water
5 tbsp oil

Beat the egg yolks and mix well with the stock. Add 2 tablespoons of the chopped ham, the bamboo shoots, wine, salt and cornflour dissolved in the water.

Beat the mixture together until it is well mixed.

Heat the oil in a wok and fry the mixture stirring continuously until thick.

Place on a serving dish, sprinkle over the remaining ham and serve hot.

STUFFED OMELETTES

Serves 6

Stuffing:
250 g/8 oz cold cooked meat (eg chicken, ham), chopped
2 tsp Chinese rice wine or dry sherry
2 tsp soy sauce
1 tsp ginger juice
¹/4 tsp salt
2 tsp cornflour
3 tbsp chopped onion

Omelettes:
3 eggs
pinch of salt
oil for frying
3 tbsp flour
3 tbsp cold water

Combine all the stuffing ingredients and divide the mixture into 6 equal portions.

Beat the eggs, adding a pinch of salt and make 6 very thin omelettes.

Place one portion of stuffing on each omelette, roll them up tightly, and seal with the flour dissolved in the water.

Deep-fry the omelettes, drain and cut each one into 5 diagonal pieces. Serve hot.

Top: Eggs Cooked in Tea
Bottom: Scrambled Egg Yolks with Bamboo Shoots

SCRAMBLED EGGS WITH PORK

Serves 6

10 tsp oil
6 eggs, beaten
2 spring onions, peeled and sliced in rings
250 g/8 oz cold cooked pork, thinly sliced
1 tbsp Chinese rice wine or dry sherry
4 tbsp soy sauce
1/2 tsp sugar

Heat 6 tablespoons oil in a frying pan, add the beaten eggs and cook, stirring continuously. Remove from the heat when the eggs are half set.

In another frying pan or wok, heat the remaining oil and fry the onions for 1-2 minutes. Add the pork, and when the meat has started to brown, ad the eggs, wine, soy sauce and sugar, mix well and serve hot.

SWEET AND SOUR EGGS

Serves 6

6 eggs
about 3 tbsp oil
1 tbsp soy sauce
1/2 tbsp wine vinegar
1/2 tbsp sugar

Heat half the oil in a frying pan and add the eggs, one at a time. When each egg sets, fold it in two to make a half moon shape and seal the edges by pressing the upper side down with the ends of chopsticks. Set each egg aside when cooked. If necessary add more oil to the pan while cooking.

When all the eggs are done, place in a frying pan with the soy sauce, vinegar and sugar. Bring to the boil and serve hot.

Top: Scrambled Eggs with Pork
Bottom: Sweet and Sour Eggs

VEGETABLES

FRIED BROAD BEANS

Serves 4

500 g/1 lb shelled broad beans
5 tbsp oil
50 ml/2 fl oz water
3 tbsp sugar
1 tbsp salt

Fry the broad beans in the oil until bright
green in colour, add the water and
seasonings, and boil for 5 minutes. Serve
hot or cold.

FRIED BAMBOO SHOOTS WITH CHINESE CABBAGE

Serves 4

350 g/12 oz bamboo shoots, finely sliced
oil for frying
1 tsp sugar
1/2 tsp salt
125 g/4 oz Chinese cabbage leaves, sliced

Cut the bamboo shoots diagonally into
thin strips, and fry until golden. Drain and
sprinkle with a little of the sugar and salt.
   Deep-fry the cabbage leaves in very hot
oil until crisp. Drain and place them on a
serving plate. Sprinkle with the remaining
sugar and salt. Place the bamboo shoots on
top and serve hot.

STEWED PUMPKIN

Serves 4

500 g/1 lb pumpkin
4 tbsp oil
1/2 tsp salt
1/2 baby onion, peeled and chopped
100 ml/4 fl oz water
2 pinches sugar

Peel the pumpkin and remove the seeds.
Cut the flesh into 5 cm/2 inch long pieces
and fry in the oil. Add the salt, chopped

onion, water and sugar. Cover and simmer
for 15 minutes. Serve hot.

**Top: Fried Bamboo Shoots with
Chinese Cabbage
Bottom: Fried Broad Beans**

GREEN PEPPERS WITH CARROT STUFFING

Serves 5

10 small green peppers
3 carrots, peeled and shredded
50 g/2 oz onion, peeled and sliced
4 tbsp oil
pinch of ground black pepper
1 tbsp sugar
100 ml/4 fl oz water
6 tbsp tomato ketchup

Cut the tops off the peppers and remove the seeds. Blanch in boiling water and refresh in cold water. Fry the carrots and onion in the oil. Add the spices and seasonings and fry a little longer.

Stuff the peppers with this mixture and place them upright in a saucepan, without the tops. Mix the tomato ketchup with the water and pour into the pan, cover and cook for 20 minutes. Serve hot.

FRIED LETTUCE

Serves 4

5 tbsp oil
1 garlic clove, peeled and crushed
400 g/14 oz lettuce leaves, washed and drained
1 tsp salt

Heat the oil and fry the garlic until brown. Add the lettuce leaves and salt and stir-fry for 1 minute.

When the lettuce leaves have turned bright green, turn into a serving dish and serve hot.

CHICKEN AND CUCUMBER SALAD WITH HOT PEPPER DRESSING

Serves 4

1/2 chicken (about 500 g/1 lb)
2 tbsp oil
1/2 cucumber, peeled
1 tsp finely sliced ginger root
5 tbsp chopped onion

Dressing:
4 tbsp sesame seeds
1 tsp sugar
3 tbsp soy sauce
3 tbsp wine vinegar
2 tbsp sesame seed oil
1/2 tsp Tabasco

Grill the chicken for 30 minutes. Remove the flesh, and chop finely. Heat the oil and

Opposite: Fried Lettuce
Above: Green Peppers with Carrot Stuffing

stir-fry the chicken for 1 minute then place on a serving dish. Cut the cucumber into long matchsticks. Mix with the chicken and sprinkle over the sliced ginger and chopped onion. Dry roast the sesame seeds and grind to a powder. Combine with the remaining dressing ingredients, mix thoroughly and pour over the chicken and cucumber just before serving.

Note: The salad tastes best if the skin of the chicken is also used. It can be prepared in advance but the dressing should be added just before serving.

CREAMY BROCCOLI

Serves 4

500 g/1 lb broccoli
3 tbs melted chicken fat or butter
200 ml/7 fl oz chicken stock
100 ml/4 fl oz full-cream evaporated milk
¹/₂ tsp salt
1 tbsp cornflour
1 tbsp chopped ham
4 mushrooms, sliced and fried

Divide the broccoli into small florets and

boil until tender. Drain well then saute in the chicken fat. Add the stock, milk and salt and bring to the boil. Stir in the cornflour, dissolved in 3 tablespoons of cold water, and mix throughly.

Pour into a serving dish, and sprinkle with the chopped ham and cooked mushrooms. Serve hot.

SPINACH SALAD

Serves 4

40 g/1¹/₂ oz dried prawns
500 g/1 lb spinach
1 tsp salt
2 tbsp sesame seed oil
2 slices thick ham, chopped
125 g/4 oz tofu, cubed

Dressing:
3 tbsp soy sauce
3 tbsp oil
3 tbsp wine vinegar

Soak the dried prawns in hot water for 20 minutes (small fesh prawns or shrimps can be substituted), then drain and chop them

Cook the spinach in boiling salted water for 3 minutes. Drain well, and chop. Place on a serving dish and sprinkle with the sesame seed oil.

Mix in the ham, prawns and tofu and chill well before serving.

Combine the dressing ingredients in a serving jug. Pour the dressing over the salad at the table and mix well.

Top: Spinach Salad
Bottom: Creamy Broccoli

AUBERGINES WITH SCRAMBLED EGGS

Serves 4

4 small aubergines, stalks removed
2 eggs, beaten
3 tbsp spring onion, chopped
3 tbsp soy sauce
1 tbsp sugar
4 tbsp oil

Steam the aubergines for about 25 minutes until tender.

Combine the eggs, chopped onion, soy sauce and sugar, and mix well. Fry this mixture in the oil, dividing it into small pieces as it sets. Cut the aubergine into chunks and arrange in a circle on a serving dish. Place the eggs in the centre and serve hot.

BRAISED TURNIPS

Serves 4

500 g/1 lb turnips, peeled
3 tbsp oil
100 ml/4 fl oz water
1 tbsp soy sauce
1/2 tsp sugar

Cut the turnips into long matchsticks. Stir-fry in the oil, add the water and seasonings, and boil for about 10 minutes. Serve hot or cold.

GREEN SWEET AND SOUR SALAD

Serves 4

1/2 cucmber, peeled
250 g/8 oz cabbage
3 small green peppers, deseeded
3 tbsp oil
4 tbsp sugar
1/2 tsp salt
2 tbsp soy sauce
3 tbsp wine vinegar

Cut the cucumber into thick matchsticks. Cut the cabbage and peppers into shreds.
   Stirfry the vegetables briefly in the oil over high heat and add the seasonings. Chill for at least 1 hour before serving.

Top: Braised Turnips
Bottom: Aubergines with Scrambled Eggs

RICE AND NOODLES

CANTONESE WHITE RICE

It is common knowledge that rice is the staple diet in southern China. It is especially popular amongst the poorer people who use it in place of bread.

White rice is prepared as follows:
Rinse it in running water until the water flowing from the rice is clear. Add the appropriate amount of water. The ratio of water to rice should be 1½:1 for long grain rice, and 2:1 for shorter grains.

Boil the rice vigorously until almost all the water is absorbed, then lower the heat, cover and simmer slowly for twenty minutes.

Rice usually doubles in volume when cooked, and if there is not enough water the rice will be too hard. Once cooked, the rice will keep for one week in the refrigerator and can be used again in fried rice dishes.

YANG CHOW RICE

Serves 4

3 tbsp oil
1 egg, beaten
150 g/5 oz cooked beef
150 g/5 oz cooked shelled prawns
50 g/2 oz shelled peas
2 spring onions, peeled and chopped
450 g/1 lb cooked rice
½ tsp salt

Heat half the oil in a frying pan or wok. Add the beaten egg and cook until set. Remove and cut into strips. Set aside.

Heat the remaining oil in a saucepan and fry the chopped beef, prawns, peas and onions for 2 minutes. Add the cooked rice and salt. Fry for 3 minutes, then mix together with the shredded egg and serve hot.

STEAMED MEAT DUMPLINGS

Serves 6

Stuffing
500 g/1 lb cooked pork or beef, chopped
1 tsp grated ginger root
3 tbsp chopped onion
6 dried mushrooms, soaked and chopped
500 g/1 lb cooked spinach, chopped
3 tbsp sesame seed oil
3 tbsp oil
4 tbsp soy sauce
1 tsp salt
1 tsp sugar
2 tbsp Chinese rice wine or dry sherry

Dumpling dough:
750 ml/1¼ pints hot water
6 tsp fresh yeast
700 g/1½ lb flour
2 tbsp sugar
½ tsp salt
3 tbsp oil

To make the stuffing, combine all the stuffing ingredients in a large mixing bowl.

For the dumpling dough, mix the water with the yeast. Add the flour and mix well. Add the remaining dough ingredients and knead until the dough is soft and elastic.

Place the dough in a mixing bowl dusted with flour, cover and leave to rise for 1½ hours in a warm place, or 3 hours at room temperature, until the dough has doubled in size.

Knead the dough on a floured surface. Roll out to about 4 cm/1½ inch thickness. Cut out 3 cm/1¼ inch rounds and flatten with the palm of your hand to 8-10 cm/3-4 inches.

Place a tablespoon of stuffing in the middle of each circle, fold the edges in and pinch together to seal. Place the dumplings in a steamer and steam for 15 - 20 minutes.

FRIED RICE WITH SOY SAUCE AND ONIONS

Serves 4

2 tbsp peanut oil
550 g/1¼ lb cold cooked rice
1 tbsp light soy sauce
1 tbsp dark soy sauce
6 baby onions, peeled and finely sliced

Heat the oil in a wok and stir-fry the rice over a high heat until the grains separate and are lightly browned. Sprinkle over the soy sauces and mix well. Add the onions, stir-fry over a high heat for 1 minute. Serve hot.

This dish may include many other ingredients, as long as they are fried separately before being added to the rice - for example: coarsely chopped ham or bacon, chopped cooked pork or Chinese sausages, cooked prawns or shrimps, shredded omelette, cooked peas etc.

Top: Yang Chow Rice
Bottom: Fried Rice with Soy Sauce and Onions

FRIED WHITE RICE

Serves 4

500 g/1 lb long grain rice
3 tbsp oil
¹/₂ tsp salt

Wash the rice, changing the water at least 4 times. Drain and place in a saucepan with enough cold water to cover the rice by about 2.5 cm/1 inch. Bring to the boil, cover and cook gently until the rice has absorbed all the water and the grains have separated. Spread the rice out in a large dish and allow to cool.

Heat the oil in a wok or frying pan and stir-fry the rice for 1-2 minutes. Remove from the heat, add salt to taste and continue stirring for a couple of minutes.

Below: Chinese Noodles
Opposite: Spring Rolls

CHINESE NOODLES

4 eggs, lightly beaten
at least 250 g/9 oz flour

Blend the beaten eggs into the flour, then knead until the dough is soft. Cover with a damp cloth and leave to stand for 20 minutes.

Knead again and roll out as thinly as possible on a floured working surface. Fold the dough onto itself 4 or 5 times and cut into the thinnest strips possible.

Most Chinese noodles are made without egg, but using the same method and the following ingredients:

250 g/9 oz strong white flour
300 ml/¹/₂ pint water
pinch of salt.

FRIED NOODLES WITH PORK AND VEGETABLES

Serves 3

250 g/8 oz Chinese noodles
5 eggs
3 tsp salt
11 tbsp oil
6 dried mushrooms, soaked and drained
2 bamboo shoots
150 g/5 oz cauliflower
250 g/8 oz spinach
1 baby onion, peeled
250 g/8 oz cooked pork, chopped
1 tbsp Chinese rice wine or dry sherry
2 tbsp soy sauce

Cook the noodles until tender, drain, refresh in cold water and drain again.

Beat the eggs with 1 teaspoon of the salt. Heat 3 tablespoons of oil in a wok or omelette pan and fry the eggs turning once. Divide the omelette into small pieces.

Cut the mushrooms, bamboo shoots, cauliflower, spinach and onion into strips. Fry all the vegetables with the pork in 3 tablespoons of the oil. Add the wine and soy sauce. Remove and reserve.

Heat the remaining oil, add the noodles and remaining salt and cook for 5 minutes, stirring constantly.

Arrange the noodles on a large serving dish, cover with the vegetables, shredded omelette and fried pork and serve piping hot.

SPRING ROLLS

Serves 4

4 tbsp oil
250 g/8 oz pork fillet, cut into thin strips
25 g/1 oz finely sliced onion
50 g/2 oz chopped dried mushrooms
1 tbsp Chinese rice wine or dry sherry
1/2 tsp salt
1 tsp cornflour
50 g/2 oz bamboo shoots, cut into matchsticks
50 g/2 oz soya sprouts

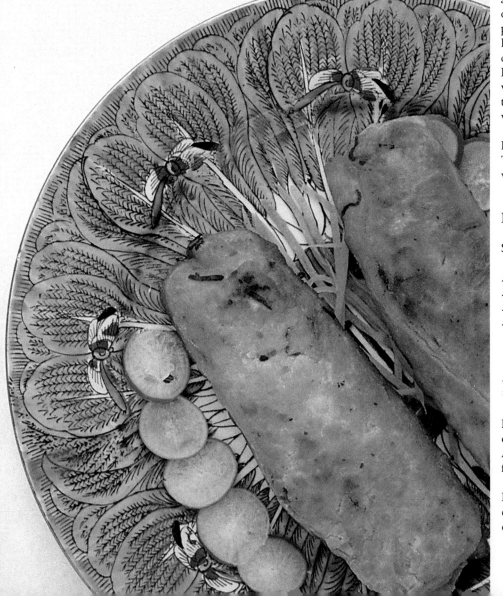

2 tbsp soy sauce

Stuffing:
Heat the oil in a frying pan or wok and stir-fry the pork, onions and mushrooms for 5 minutes. Add the remaining ingredients and mix well. Remove from the heat and leave to cool.

Pancake coating:
200 g/7 oz flour
2 eggs, lightly beaten
3/4 litre/1 1/4 pints water
knob of butter
oil for frying

There are various methods for making the coating, but the following is the simplest:

Place the flour in a mixing bowl. Make a well in the centre, add the eggs and mix into the flour, gradually adding the water to make a smooth batter.

Grease a 18 cm/7 inch frying pan with the butter, and add a little oil. Pour a little batter into the pan, spreading it out to make a very thin sheet. Cook on one side until golden then remove from the pan and keep aside; in China the panckaes are only cooked on one side. Repeat the process until all the batter has been used. Place 2 tablespoons of the stuffing in the centre of the cooked side of each pancake. Brush the edges with a little cornflour and water to paste, and roll up the pancakes tightly. Deepfry the rolls, and serve hot with soy sauce.

Note:
The pork in the filling may be substituted with beef, chicken or prawns.

RICE WITH MINCED PORK

Serves 4

2 tbsp oil
250 g/8 oz minced pork
3 spring onions, peeled and chopped
2.5 cm/1 inch ginger root, finely sliced
1 garlic clove, peeled and crushed
1 tbsp soy sauce
1 small green pepper, deseeded and chopped
450 g/1 lb long grain rice, rinsed
1/2 tsp salt

Heat the oil in a wok and stir-fry the pork, onions, ginger, and garlic for 5 minutes. Add the soy sauce and green pepper and fry for another 5 minutes.

Place the rice in a saucepan and add enough water to cover the rice by 2 cm/3/4 inch. Add the salt and cook until all the water has been absorbed and the rice is half cooked. Scatter the minced pork over the rice, cover and cook gently for 6-8 minutes. Remove from the heat. Mix the meat and rice thoroughly. Serve hot, and provide a mixture of salt and freshly ground black pepper to be added to taste.

Top: Rice with Minced Pork
Bottom: Egg Fried Rice with Prawns

EGG FRIED RICE WITH PRAWNS

Serves 4

500 g/1 lb long grain rice
2 eggs
3 tbsp oil
2 spring onions, peeled and chopped
1 large onion, peeled and chopped
1 garlic clove, peeled and crushed
100 g/4 oz shelled cooked prawns
1/2 tsp salt
2 tbsp soy sauce
60 g/2 1/2 oz cooked peas

Wash the rice in several changes of water. Place in a saucepan and add enough water to cover by 2.5 cm/1 inch. Bring to the boil, stir once and reduce the heat. Cover and cook gently until the rice is dry and has absorbed all the water. Remove from the heat, cover with cold water and drain well. Spread out the rice in a large dish and separate the grains carefully with a fork.

Beat the eggs with a large pinch of salt. Heat 1 tablespoon of the oil in a saucepan and stir-fry the chopped onions for 2 minutes. Add the beaten eggs and stir until scrambled. Turn into a mixing bowl and set aside.

Heat another tablespoon of the oil and fry the crushed garlic for a few seconds, then add the prawns and stir-fry for 1 minute. Remove and set aside. Heat the reamining spoon of oil and fry the rice with the salt until heated right through. Add the soy sauce, prawns, eggs and peas, stir well to mix the ingredients. Serve at once while piping hot.

SOUPS

CREAM OF CHICKEN SOUP WITH CORN

Serves 1

125 g/4 oz chicken breast, chopped
1 tbsp Chinese rice wine or dry sherry
1/2 tsp salt
2 egg whites, lightly beaten
1/4 litre/7 fl oz chicken stock
2 tbsp sweetcorn purée
1 tbsp cornflour
3 tbsp water
1 tbsp chopped ham

Mix the chopped chicken with the wine, 1 teaspoon of the salt and the lightly beaten egg whites.

Heat the chicken stock in a saucepan, add the chicken mixture, the sweetcorn purée and the remaining salt and bring to the boil. Then add the cornflour mixed with the water. Cook for 3 minutes, stirring continuously, until the soup thickens.

Pour into a soup tureen and garnish with chopped ham. Serve hot.

CHICKEN AND SPINACH SOUP

Serves 4

250 g/8 oz boneless chicken breast
3 slices ginger root
1 onion, peeled and sliced
25 g/1 oz dried egg noodles
250 g/8 oz spinach, roughly shredded
pinch of salt
1 tbsp Chinese rice wine or dry sherry

Place the chicken, ginger and sliced onion in a saucepan. Cover with cold water, bring to the boil, cover and simmer for at least 1 hour. Strain, reserving the stock and the chicken.

Cook the noodles, drain and chop. Bring the stock to boil, add the spinach, noodles and remaining ingredients and cook until the spinach is done. Chop the cooked chicken and add to the soup. Serve piping hot.

MIXED MEAT SOUP

Serves 4

2 1/4 pints/1.2 litres water
100 g/4 oz boneless chicken breast, finely diced
100 g/4 oz pork tenderloin, finely diced
100 g/4 oz ham, diced
75 g/3 oz bamboo shoots, diced
4 dried mushrooms, soaked, de-stalked and diced
100 g/4 oz shelled cooked prawns
6 scallops
50 g/2 oz chopped green vegetables
2 tsp salt
2 tsp Chinese rice wine or dry sherry

Left: Chicken and Spinach Soup
Right: Cream of Chicken Soup with Corn

Heat the water in a saucepan until boiling. Add all the other ingredients, return to the boil then cover and simmer for 15 minutes. Serve piping hot.

EGG AND CUCUMBER SOUP

Serves 6

2 tbsp oil
250 g/8 oz pork tenderloin, cut into strips
1/2 onion, peeled and diced
2 tsp soy sauce
2 tsp cornflour
2.3 litres/4 pints chicken stock
2 tsp Chinese rice wine or dry sherry
1/2 cucumber finely sliced
1 tbsp salt

Heat the oil in a large saucepan and brown the pork and onion. Add the soy sauce and cornflour. Stir well, add the stock and wine and bring to the boil. Add the cucumber and salt.

Lightly beat the eggs, and slowly pour into the soup, stirring gently so the eggs form flower shapes as they set.

Note: The pork may be substituted with chicken breast or fillet of beef.

Below, top: **Mixed Meat Soup**
Below, bottom: **Egg and Cucumber Soup**
Opposite, top: **Fruit Salad with Almond Jelly**
Opposite, bottom: **Almond Custard**

SWEET DISHES

FRUIT SALAD WITH ALMOND JELLY

Serves 6

15 g/1½ oz gelatine
1 litre/2 pints water
6 tbsp full cream evaporated milk
2 tsp almond essence
1 medium can mixed fruit salad

Soak the gelatine in a little of the water. Heat until dissolved, add the remaining water and bring to the boil. Add the milk and almond essence and mix well.

Pour into a large dish and allow the jelly to set slightly, then place in the refrigerator. When the jelly has set completely, cut into blocks and mix with the fruit salad. Serve well chilled.

ALMOND CUSTARD

Serves 6

900 ml/1½ pints water
4 tsp agar-agar
1 small can full-cream evaporated milk
2 tsp almond essence

Bring the water to the boil, sprinkle in the agar-agar and stir until dissolved. Add the milk and almond essence and mix thoroughly. Pour into a fairly shallow mould and chill until set. Just before serving, cut into blocks or cubes and serve on its own or decorated with canned fruit or melon balls.

FULL MOON DESSERT

Serves 6

125 g/4 oz sesame seeds
250 g/8 oz sugar
250 g/8 oz lard
350 g/12 oz rice flour

This dessert is very popular in the southern regions of China, and traditionally it is eaten on the day of the first full moon in January.

Below: Full Moon Dessert
Opposite: Sweet Potato Balls

Wash the sesame seeds and, without drying them, roast in a wok with no fat; be careful, as sesame seeds burn very easily. Crush the seeds in a mortar, then mix with the sugar and lard to make little cherry-sized balls. Set aside to firm up.

Mix the rice flour with enough water to make a soft dough. Knead lightly and divide into balls about 4 cm/1½ inches in diameter. Place one sesame seed ball in the middle of each flour ball and fold the dough around the smaller ball until it is completely enclosed.

Poach the balls in boiling water, moving them constantly until they rise to the surface, then allow to cook for a few minutes. Serve hot in the water they are cooked in. If desired, garnish with walnuts, canned fruit, sweet soya bean paste or sesame seeds.

SWEET POTATO BALLS

Serves 6

500 g/1 lb sweet potatoes, peeled and cubed
8 tbsp sugar
1 egg, beaten
2 tbsp flour
6 tbsp water
40 g/1½ oz sesame seeds
oil for frying

Steam the sweet potato until tender, then purée. Leave to cool, add the sugar and egg and stir until well blended. Form the mixture into balls using a tablespoon. Mix the flour with the water, and roll the balls first in this paste, then in the sesame seeds. Fry the balls for a few seconds, just long enough for the sesame seeds to turn light brown. Serve hot.

INTRODUCTION
Japanese Cuisine

Japanese cuisine differs greatly from other Asian cuisines in the simplicity of its dishes and cooking methods. It is distinguised not by the spices used nor by the rich exotic flavours of the dishes, but instead by the emphasis placed on the quality of the basic ingredients. Attention is given to highlighting the natural appearance of the food, its original flavour and individual qualities, and these are never masked by sophisticated seasonings or strong spices. Perhaps this is the reason why people accustomed to eating dishes with rich sauces and subtle blends of flavours are sometimes surprised and slightly disappointed by the simplicity of Japanese dishes. However, as one becomes more accustomed to Japanese cookery, one learns to appreciate its qualities, for, indeed, it deserves the respect of all true *gourmands*.

A westerner looking at Japanese dishes cannot fail to see that they are a labour of love. The exquisite presentation of the "ikebana", for example, enhances the natural appearance of its ingredients, and the food is arranged with such perfect simplicity that this style of cooking could almost be defined as a form of art.

A Japanese chef does not see his creations as mere sustenance, but rather as expressions of spirituality. The colour of the serving plates, the sparse decoration of the table and a calm atmosphere all combine to create a environment that delights the senses.

The Japanese value the quality of their dishes very highly, particularly for food that is in season, the "market cooking" that so many modern western chefs talk about. In Japan, for example,

the first strawberries or mushrooms of the season are like precious jewels.

The most common cooking process in Japan is braising or steaming; in fact, the delivate flavour and lightness that this lends to food is one of the main characteristics of Japanese cookery.

Lightness is also sought after in fried food; "tonkatsu" and "tempura", for example, are easy to digest. For frying, the Japanese use vegetable oils, usually a blend of corn, olive and sesame oils. The sesame oil adds flavour. The oil is always heated to the right temperature so that the food being fried does not become greasy and heavy.

"Tempura" is one of the best known Japanese dishes in the West. This delicious fried fish dish was introduced by the Portuguese in the 16th century to compensate for their abstinence from meat during Lent.

"Tonkatsu" is a pork dish introduced by the Germans as a replacement for their own "Wiener Schnitzel," and fried chicken is also a foreign dish, originating in China. However, the Japanese have made all of these dishes taste deliciously different to the way they taste in their countries of origin.

No-one can compete with Japanese chefs when it comes to presentation, for they have an instinctive feeling for decoration and simplicity. In their creations there is always one tiny detail, a flower, a blade of grass, or something intended to portray the current season. The Japanese refuse to eat any food that is not in its natural season.

Knowing how to cook rice is fundamental and any Japanese chef must be able to produce perfectly cooked rice. The method for cooking rice can be found in this book under the appropriate heading.

In Chinese cuisine the presentation often becomes a show, as diverse delicious dishes are served concurrently. Smilarly, in Japanese cuisine, the diner receives an individual tray on which all the dishes are served at once, with each dish in a carefully selected bowl or dish. Soup is served in bowls with lids; these lacquer containers keep the soup hot for a long time, but must be handled with care, for the water vapour acts as a suction pump and makes the lid stick to the rim of the bowl.

Chopsticks are the normal eating implements, and are used to pick up all the solid pieces in soups, after which the bowl is raised to the mouth in both hands. The Japanese never use spoons, except to eat "chawn moshi", a salty steamed flan.

Although rice is of prime importance, it can easily be substituted by noodles.

"Sake" or tea are served with a meal; in the summer, the Japanese usually drink a very refreshing barley infusion called "mugicha". In the winter, the "sake" bottle is put in hot water to warm it up and is drunk from tiny cups called "sakazuki". It may also be served frozen in summer.

Left: Bream Soup
Right: Chicken Stock

SOUPS

BREAM SOUP

Serves 4

6 small bream (50 g/2 oz each), filleted
salt
8 uncooked prawns
50 g/2 oz Shungiku (Japanese vegetable)
8 rice balls: 4 white and 4 red
2.3 litres/4 pints Dashi (basic stock)
8 button mushrooms, sliced
2 bamboo shoots, sliced
soy sauce to taste

Bream is a freshwater fish, about
8-10 cm/3-4 inches long, weighing about
50 g/2 oz. It is highly esteemed by the
Japanese for its taste. If bream is
unavailable, substitute any other small
whole fish. Rub the fish with salt, then
leave for 15 minutes.

Rinse then cook in a large pan of
simmering salted water, taking care that
the fish remains whole. Remove from the
pan and drain well.

Shell the prawns, leaving on the tails,
and sprinkle with salt. Cook in boiling
salted water until they turn pink, then
drain.

Scald the shungiku in boiling water.
Drain, pat dry and cut into 2.5 cm/1 inch
lengths.

Toast the rice balls until they start to
brown.

Place ½ litre/¾ pint of the stock in a
saucepan. Add the fish and all the
vegetables, except the shungiku, and heat
through. Heat the remaining stock in
another saucepan. Add salt and soy sauce
to taste.

Place the vegetables and fish in
individual serving bowls, add the shungiku
and pour over the hot stock. Serve piping
hot.

CHICKEN STOCK

Makes about 1.7 litres/3 pints

½ a whole chicken and the bones of the other
half
3 large pieces of ginger root
1½ tsp salt
1.7 litres/3 pints water
2 spring onions.

Place the chicken half and the bones in a
large saucepan with the remaining
ingredients and bring to the boil. Cover
and simmer for at least 1 hour, whisking
from time to time. Leave to cool, strain
through muslin an chill in the refrigerator
so the grease can be scraped off the
surface. This stock should be completley
clear and can be used when Dashi is not
available (see recipe below).

DASHI (SOUP BASE)

Dashi is one of the most basic ingredients
in Japanese cookery. It is very easy to
make and will keep in the refrigerator for a
couple of days. Commercially produced
Dashi is sold in sachets.
Makes about 2.3 litres/2½ pints

5 cm/2 inches kombu (dried seaweed)
⅔ litres/2½ pints water
3 tbsp katsuobushi (bonito flakes)

Wash the seaweed in cold water. Bring the
water to the boil, add the seaweed, stir
well and boil for 3 minutes. Remove the
seaweed, add the bonito flakes to the
water, bring back to the boil and remove
from the heat. Leave to stand for a few
minutes to allow the pices of bonito to
sink to the bottom. After straining, the
dashi will be ready to use.

FISH SOUP

Serves 4

500 g/1 lb mixed fish bones and trimmings
2.3 litres/2½ pints water
2 pieces ginger root
1 small onion, peeled and quartered
1 tbsp Japanese soy sauce
1 tbsp sake
1 tsp salt
3 tbsp chopped spring onion
4 slices raw fish (optional)

Place the fish bones and trimmings in a
saucepan with the water, ginger and onion
quarters. Bring to the boil and cook gently
for 15 minutes, stirring occasionally.

Leave to cool and strain. Add the soy
sauce, sake and salt.

Just before serving, reheat the soup, add
the chopped onion, then remove from the
heat and serve immediately. You may also
put a thin slice of raw fish in each bowl
before pouring in the soup.

VEGETABLE SOUP

Serves 6

½ litre/¾ pint Dashi (see recipe on this page)
1 tsp salt
1 tsp Japanese soy sauce
8 eggs
100 g/4 oz spinach
2 thin slices lemon, cut in small pieces

Season the stock with the salt and soy
sauce, and bring to the boil.

Poach the eggs in boiling salted water
until the yolks are lightly set.

Remove the eggs with a slotted spoon,
place on a tea towel and leave to drain.
Blanch the spinach leaves in salted water,
then refresh in cold water. Place the eggs
in soup bowls, add the spinach, and the
the stock and garnish with small pieces of
lemon.

Top: Dashi (recipe on page 49)
Bottom: Vegetable Soup (recipe on
page 49)

RICE AND NOODLES

RICE WITH CHICKEN AND MUSHROOMS (OBORO)

Serves 6

8 dried mushrooms (shiitake)
550 g/1¼ lb short grain rice
4 tbsp mirin or dry sherry
2 tbsp sugar
4 tbsp Japanese soy sauce
400 g/14 oz boneless chicken breast, chopped
2 eggs, beaten
pinch of salt
175 g/6 oz cooked peas

Soak the dried mushrooms in boiling water for 30 minutes. Drain, reserving the liquid, and remove the stalks.

Wash the rice carefully and leave to drain in a sieve for 30 minutes. Cook in boiling, salted water while preparing the rest of the dish.

Place the mushroom heads in a small saucepan with half the soaking liquid and half the wine and sugar. Bring to the boil, cover and cook until almost all the liquid has evaporated. Remove from the heat and leave to cool.

Add the remaining wine and sugar to the pan with the soy sauce and 50 ml/2 fl oz of the mushroom soaking liquid. Add the chopped chicken, cover and cook very gently for 3 minutes. Remove from the heat and keep covered.

Season the eggs with the salt and make 2-3 large thin omelettes, removing them from the pan before they turn golden. Cut into strips.

Place the drained cooked rice in a large serving dish. Scatter over the chicken and sprinkle with the cooking liquid left in the saucepan. Slice the mushroom heads and scatter on top. Decorate with the strips of omelette and cooked peas.
Serve hot.

Top: Domburi (recipe on page 52)
Bottom: Rice with Chicken and Mushrooms (Oboro)

DOMBURI

A "Domburi" is an earthenware bowl, but the term is also used to describe the food it contains.

Serves 6

175 g/6 oz short grain rice
1/2 litre/3/4 pint chicken stock
3 tbsp mirin or dry sherry
5 tbsp Japanese soy sauce
1 chicken breast and 1 thigh, skinned, boned and diced
6 eggs, beaten
2 pinches salt
6 spring onions, peeled and chopped

Cook the rice following the traditional Gohan recipe (see page 54) and keep hot.

Place the chicken stock in a saucepan with the wine and soy sauce and bring to the boil.

Add the diced chicken, bring back to the boil, cover and cook for 8 minutes. Season the beaten eggs with salt and add to the chicken stock with the chopped onion. Bring to the boil again, but be careful not to stir. Cover and cook very gently for 3-4 minutes, until the eggs have started to set, but are still soft.

Place the rice in an earthenware bowl and pour over the egg and chicken mixture. Serve at once while piping hot.

FRIED CHICKEN WITH RICE

Serves 6

1 small chicken, jointed
100 ml/4 fl oz Japanese soy sauce
100 ml/4 fl oz mirin or dry sherry
2 cloves garlic, peeled and crushed
1 tsp grated ginger root
550 g/1 1/4 lb short grain rice
50 ml/2 fl oz oil
100 g/4 oz Chinese mushrooms (or other fresh mushrooms), sliced
3/4 litre/1 1/4 pints chicken stock (page 49)
3 tsp sugar
3 spring onions, peeled and finely chopped
50 g/2 oz peas

Marinate the chicken pieces for 30 minutes in a mixture of the soy sauce, wine, garlic and ginger.

Wash and drain the rice, and cook according to the traditional Gohan recipe (see page 54). Drain the chicken and reserve the marinade.

Heat the oil and fry the chicken pieces over medium heat until cooked through. Leave to cool a little then cut the flesh into bite-size pieces. Add the mushrooms to the pan and fry briefly.

Place the rice and chicken in a deep serving bowl. Mix the marinade with the stock, add the sugar and bring to the boil.

Left: Fried Noodles in Dashi Sauce
Opposite: Fried Chicken with Rice

Add the onions, peas and mushrooms, return to the boil then pour over the rice. Serve at once, garnished with small strips of omelette if desired.

FRIED NOODLES IN DASHI SAUCE

Serves 4

200 g/7 oz buckwheat noodles (soba)
1 sheet seaweed (nori)
1 tbsp grated ginger root
3 spring onions, peeled and chopped

Sauce:
1/2 litre/3/4 pint Dashi (page 49)
100 ml/4 fl oz Japanese soy sauce
100 ml/4 fl oz mirin or dry sherry
salt or sugar to taste

Bring a pan of water to the boil. Add the noodles and bring back to the boil. Add 225 ml/8 fl oz cold water and leave for 2 minutes until the noodles are "al dente". Drain, rinse under running water and drain again thoroughly.

Place the nori on a baking tray or grill pan and toast under the grill until crisp. Place the noodles on a serving dish and crumble over the grilled nori.

Combine all the sauce ingredients in a small saucepan and bring to the boil. Remove from the heat and leave to cool. The sauce can be savoury or sweet as preferred.

Mix the ginger and chopped onion together, and place a small portion of the mixture on individual plates. Pour the sauce into individual cups. Serve the noodles with the onion mixture and sauce as seasoning.

RICE BALLS (MUSUBI)

In Japan rice is sometimes served in the form of very appetizing little balls made in the following way:

Cook the rice and set aside until lukewarm. Take about 75 g/3 oz of the rice and squeeze tightly to make the balls. These can be flavoured with various seasonings, the most common being "gomasio", a very popular Japanese condiment, which is a mixture of black sesame seeds, rock salt and a little monosodium glutamate. Also cooked rice may be wrapped around raw or smoked fish, cut into very thin strips. "Nori" (dried seaweed), considered to be an indispensable condiment, is often used to flavour rice balls.

WHITE RICE (GOHAN)

In Japanese cuisine rice is served with every meal. Short or medium grain white rice is preferred, since the grains tend to stick together and are easier to pick up with chopsticks.

Serves 6

550 g/1¼ lb short or medium grain rice
3/4 litre/1¼ pints water

Wash the rice in serveral changes of water, then leave to drain for at least 30 minutes. Place the rice in a saucepan with water, cover and bring to the boil. Reduce the heat and cook very gently, still covered, for 15 minutes.

Increase the heat and cook at a very high temperature, still covered, for another twenty seconds. Remove from the heat and wait 10 minutes before serving.

FRIED RICE WITH TOFU (KITSUNE)

Serves 6

425 g/15 oz cooked short grain rice
2 slices tofu, fried
600 ml/1 pint Dashi (page 49) or chicken stock
100 ml/4 fl oz soy sauce
100 ml/4 fl oz mirin or dry sherry
1 tbsp sugar
6 spring onions, peeled and finely chopped

Cook the rice as for Gohan rice. Meanwhile, cut the tofu into matchstick size pieces.

Pour the stock, soy sauce and wine into a saucepan, add the tofu and sugar and bring to the boil. Cook gently for 10 minutes, then add the onions. Cover and boil for 1 minute. Place the rice in a large serving bowl or 6 individual bowls and pour over the boiling soup. Serve piping hot.

SWEET RICE WITH VINEGAR (SUSHI)

Serves 6

550 g/1¼ lb medium or short grain rice
3/4 litre/1¼ pints water

Sauce:
4 tbsp vinegar
3 tbsp sugar
2½ tsp salt
2 tbsp mirin or dry sherry

Wash the rice in several changes of water and leave to drain for 30 minutes.

Place the rice in a saucepan with the water, cover and bring to the boil. Cook gently for 15 minutes without removing the lid.

Remove from the heat and leave for 10 minutes, still covered. Combine thoroughly all the ingredients for the sauce. Place the rice in a large bowl, pour over the sauce and mix well. Leave to cool to room temperature before serving.

SEAFOOD

KUCHITORI

Serves 6

Tazunazushi:
7 eggs
1/2 tsp salt
1 tbsp sugar
100 ml/4 fl oz vinegar
4 Dublin Bay prawns (langoustines), cooked or
raw (see recipe)
8 whiting fillets

Beat the eggs with the salt and sugar. Use the mixture to make scrambled eggs, then sieve and leave to cool. Stir in 1¹/₂ tablespoons of the vinegar. If using uncooked Dublin Bay prawns, open from the back, without removing the spine. Thread onto skewers and cook in salted water (the skewers prevent the prawns from rolling around while cooking.). When the prawns change colour, remove from the water and allow to cool. Peel the cooked prawns and split in half lengthways. Combine the ingredients for the marinade and marinate the prawns for 12 hours. Sprinkle a little salt over the fish fillets and leave for 2 hours. Wash and dry the fillets then marinate in the remaining vinegar for 30 minutes.

Line a cake tin with greased greaseproof paper and place alternating layers of prawns and whiting diagonally across the tin. Place the scrambled eggs on top and press down. Cover the tin and weight down. Chill for 3 hours, then turn out of the tin and cut into slices 2.5 cm/1 inch thick slices.

The whiting fillets may be substituted with thinly sliced fish steaks and served separately from the prawns.

Chicken:
2 chicken wings
1 tbsp oil
1 lemon, halved lengthways, sliced

Marinade:
2 tbsp Japanese soy sauce
2 tbsp mirin or dry sherry

Marinate the chicken in the soy sauce and mirin for 3 hours. Drain and fry the chicken in the hot oil, stirring until

Top: Kuchitori
Bottom: Teriyaki (recipe on page 56)

cooked. Dip in the marinade again then allow to cool. Slice the chicken thinly and arrange on the kuchitori serving dish with slices of lemon.

Asparagus and sesame seeds:

500 g/1 lb asparagus, cooked
2 tbsp vinegar
1 tsp sugar
1 tbsp soy sauce
3 tbsp sesame seeds
1/2 tsp salt

Arrange the asparagus on the Kuchitori serving dish. Combine the remaining ingredients and pour over the asparagus.

TERIYAKI

Serves 6

1 kg/2.2 lb fish (eg mackerel, herring), filleted

Marinade:
100 ml/4 fl oz mirin or dry sherry
5 tbsp soy sauce
1 tsp poppy seeds
50 g/2 oz ginger root, grated

Cut the fish fillets into large chunks. Combine the ingredients for the marinade, and marinate the fish for 2 hours.

Drain the fish from the marinade and grill under moderate heat until tender. Sprinkle the poppy seeds and grated ginger over the fish while still hot.

Separated eggs:
4 hard-boiled eggs, halved
sugar
salt

Scoop out the egg yolks and sieve into a bowl. Stir in 1 tablespoon of sugar and 1/2 teaspoon salt. Sieve the egg whites into another bowl and stir in 1 teaspoon sugar and a pinch of salt. Heap the whites on a damp serviette in a rectangle about 10 cm x 15 cm/4 in x 6 in. Spread the yolks across the top of the whites, cover with another serviette and tie. Place the package in a steamer and steam over a high heat for 10 minutes. Allow to cool, and cut into small pieces.

Mint jelly:

Makes 3/4 litre/1 1/4 pints

1 piece agar-agar
250 g/8 oz sugar

few drops of mint essence
few drops of green food colouring

Soak the agar-agar in water, drain and cut into small chunks. Place in a saucepan with the water and heat until the agar-agar has dissolved. Add the sugar and continue cooking until the liquid has reduced by half. Add the mint essence and green food colouring. Mix well and strain into a shallow dish to come 1 cm/1/2 inch up the sides. Leave to set. Turn out onto a board and cut into flower shapes with a pastry cutter. Finally, arrange the fish, eggs and mint jelly on a serving dish, and serve.

CRAB WITH CUCUMBER

Serves 6

1 small cucumber, finely sliced
salt to taste
6 tbsp wine vinegar
1 tbsp sugar
150 g/15 oz canned crab meat
slice of ginger root, finely chopped

Place the cucumber slices in a colander, sprinkle with salt and leave for 20 minutes to draw out the excess moisture. Drain well, place in a mixing bowl and stir in 1 1/2 tablespoons of the vinegar. Combine the remaining vinear with the sugar. Soak the ginger in water for a few minutes to take away the sharpness, and drain. Arrange the crab and cucumber on a serving dish and garnish with the ginger.

TEMPURA

Serves 4

16 medium-sized uncooked prawns
500 g/1 lb fish fillets
1 lotus root
1 medium can miniature corn cobs
3 preserved bamboo shoots
2-3 gingko nuts
1 spring onion, peeled
250 g/8 oz mushrooms
1 tbsp grated mouli (daihon)
2 tbsp grated ginger root
1/2 litre/3/4 pint oil
100 ml/4 fl oz sesame seed oil

Batter:
1 egg
225ml/8 fl oz iced water
125 g/4 oz flour
pinch of bicarbonate of soda

Sauce:
3 tbsp mirin or dry sherry
3 tbsp Japanese soy sauce
pinch of salt

Shell the prawns, but do not remove the tails. Wash and drain on kitchen towels. Slice the fish fillets into strips. Drain the canned vegetables on kitchen towels. Thinly slice the lotus root and bamboo shoots into rounds, and if the latter are quite thick, cut each slice in half.

Stick the gingko nuts on a chopstick or toothpick. Chop the onion. Cut the mushrooms into 2 or 3 chunks, depending on their size.

Arrange all the ingredients on a serving dish, cover and chill until serving time

Place before each diner a small plate covered with a paper serviette, a small bowl of sauce and another bowl filled with a mixture of the grated mouli and ginger.

Prepare the sauce. Make the batter shortly before using it, and keep in a bowl placed in a larger bowl filled with ice Heat the oils together to about 190°C/375°F.

When the guests are at the table, dip the pieces of vetgetable, fish and prawns in the batter, one at a time, and fry them in the hot oil; take care not to fry more than 6 pieces at a time, or the oil will not be hot enough. As soon as the batter is golden, remove the fritters and drain immediately on kitchen towels. Serve at once.

The guests can dip the fritters in the sauce and eat them while they are still hot and crisp, adding mouli and ginger to taste.

Batter:
Break the egg into a bowl containing the iced water and whisk until frothy. Add the flour and bicarbonate of soda and beat until the flour is incorporated. Do not overbeat.

The batter should be very thin. If necessary, add a few drops of iced water.

Sauce
Heat the wine in a small saucepan. Remove from the heat and set it alight, moving the pan until the flame goes out. Add the remaining ingredients and bring to the boil. Leave to cool to room temperature. Finally, taste to check the seasoning.

Top: Tempura
Bottom: Crab with Cucumber

FISH AND VEGETABLE PARCELS

Serves 4

1 tbsp sake
1/2 tsp salt
4 white fish fillets
8 prawns
12 gingko nuts
4 large dried mushrooms

Soak the mushrooms in hot water for 30 minutes, then remove the stalks and slice the heads.

Mix together the sake and salt in a large shallow dish. Marinate the fish fillets in the mixture for 10 minutes. Remove the heads of the prawns and split the shell in two to extract the black vein from the back without removing the shell.

Cut out 8 pieces of aluminum foil large enough to take the fish. Lightly grease with oil. Place on each sheet 1 fish fillet, 2 prawns, 1 sliced mushroom and 3 gingko nuts. Fold the foil sheet around the contents and bake in the overn at 170°C/325°F/gas mark 3 for 20 minutes.

The foil parcels may also be cooked on a barbecue.

GRILLED MARINATED FISH

Seves 4

2 tuna steaks (or thickly sliced mackerel)
4 tbsp Japanese soy sauce
2 tbsp mirin or dry sherry
2 tbsp sake
2 tsp grated ginger root
1 tbsp sugar

Garnish:
1 very small cucumber
3 tbsp white wine vinegar
3 tbsp sugar
1 tsp Japanese soy sauce
1 tsp salt

Cut each piece of fish into 4 pieces.
Combine the soy sauce, wine and sake.
Squeeze out the juice from the ginger into
this mixture and stir in the sugar until
dissolved. Marinate the fish in the mixture
for 30 minutes.
Grill or dry fry the fish until tender.
Decorate with the garnish ingredients.

Opposite: Grilled Marinated Fish
Below: Fish and Vegatable Parcels

MEAT AND POULTRY

SUKIYAKI

Serves 6

700 g/1¹/₂ lb beef sirloin
12 leeks
25 g/1 oz clear noodles (shiritaki)
2 slices tofu
500 g/1 lb shungiku, chopped
16 mushrooms, sliced
1 large carrot, peeled and sliced
a little lard or butter

Warishita sauce:
³/₄ litre/1¹/₄ pints Dashi (basic stock) (page 49)
350 ml/12 fl oz soy sauce
12 tbsp sugar

Cut the steak into small pieces. Slice the leeks into 5 cm/2 inch lengths. Scald the clear noodles in boiling water. Rinse and drain then cut into 6 cm/2¹/₄ inch lengths. Cut the tofu into 4 cm/1¹/₂ inch cubes and

Left: Shabu-Shabu
Right: Sukiyaki

toast lightly. Place all the sukiyaki ingredients in a large dish.

Combine all the sauce ingredients and bring to the boil.

Sukiyaki is traditionally cooked at the table; use an electric frying pan or table-top gas burner. Rub the pan with a little fat and heat gently. Add some vegetables and a little meat and cook gently. Repeat the process until all the meat and vegetables are cooked, frying in small batches. Add the toasted tofu and sauce as required. At first the flavour will seem light, but in the course of cooking the flavours will intensify so there is no need to add seasoning. Serve in bowls of rice.

Sukiyaki is often served with beaten raw egg in a separate bowl. Each guest can dip the meat and vegetables in the egg to enhance the taste.

SHABU-SHABU

Serves 6

2 tbsp wasabi or English mustard
juice of 1 lemon
100 ml/4 fl oz tomato ketchup
2 tbsp Japanese soy sauce
50 g/2 oz chopped leeks
50 g/2 oz ginger root, grated
5 tbsp sesame seeds, toasted
1¹/₂ litre/2¹/₂ pints Dashi (page 49)
1 kg/2.2 lb beef fillet or sirloin, finely sliced
10 mushrooms
250 g/8 oz hungiku
1 carrot, sliced and blanched
¹/₂ bamboo shoot, sliced
250 g/¹/₂ lb tofu, cubed
170 g/6 oz noodles, cooked

Place the wasabi and lemon juice in small bowls in the centre of the table. Place the soy sauce, tomato ketchup, chopped leeks and grated ginger in individual bowls as dipping sauces for each guest. Grind the sesame seeds, and add some stock, drop by drop, until a smooth paste is formed. This

should also be served as a dipping sauce.

Place an electric frying pan or table-top gas burner in the centre of the table and heat the remaining stock. Place the remaining ingredients (except the noodles) on a serving dish and dip into the hot stock, using chopsticks. When the meat and vegetables are cooked, reheat the noodles in the stock to finish off the meal.

BRAISED CHICKEN WITH VEGETABLES

Serves 6

1 x 1 kg/2.2 lb chicken
1.4 litres /2½ pints water plus 3 tbsp
2 tbsp salt
250 g/8 oz bamboo shoots
1 large carrot, sliced
1 broccoli floret
8 mushrooms

Cut the chicken into medium-size pieces. Place in a flameproof casserole, add the water, cover and simmer for 30 minutes until the meat comes off the bone easily.

Place the bamboo shoots in a saucepan and heat through gently. Drain and chop. Place the carrots in a saucepan with enough water to cover. Add the bamboo shoots and broccoli, cover and simmer until the carrots are just tender. Add the mushrooms. Mix the cornflour with the remaining water and stir into the saucepan. Cook until thickened and serve immediately with the chicken.

SWEET AND SPICY PORK
Serves 6

225 g/8 oz rice bran
1 kg/2.2 lb pork fillet in one piece
80 g/3½ oz sugar
1 tsp egg white
100 ml/4 fl oz mirin or dry sherry
8 tbsp soy sauce

Bring a large saucepan of water to the boil, add the rice bran and simmer for 20 minutes. Drain and set aside.

Wrap the pork fillet in greased aluminium foil and bake in the oven at 190°C/375°F/gas mark 5 for about 1½ hours until very tender. Remove from the oven and leave to cool in the foil. When

cold, cut the meat into 8 pieces.

Meanwhile, combine 2 litre/3¼ pints of water, sugar and egg white in a saucepan. Bring to the boil, whisking until the liquid is smooth. Strain to remove the froth and leave to cool.

When the sauce is cold, add the wine, soy sauce and finally the meat. Cover the

saucepan and bring to the boil. Cook until three quarters of the liquid has evaporated, skimming the fat and froth off the top. Season, transfer to a serving dish and serve with the rice bran.

Top: Braised Chicken with Vegetables
Bottom: Sweet and Spicy Pork

OTHER DISHES

SWEET RED BEANS

Serves 6

400 g/14 oz aduki beans
350 g/12 oz sugar
1 tsp salt

Wash and drain the beans and soak in plenty of cold water overnight. Drain the beans, place in a large saucepan and cover generously with cold water. Add the sugar, bring to the boil and simmer for about 20 minutes. Add the salt, cover and set aside for 24 hours. Drain well and serve.

VEGETABLES WITH SCRAMBLED EGGS AND PRAWNS

Serves 6

1/2 cucumber, finely sliced
400 g/14 oz daikon (white radish) or small turnips, peeled and finely sliced
2 carrots, peeled and finely sliced
3 tsp salt
5 dried mushrooms
4 1/2 tbsp vinegar
250 g/8 oz uncooked prawns
3 eggs, lightly beaten
2 1/2 tsp sugar

Place the shredded cucumber, sliced daikon and carrots in a colander. Sprinkle over 1 1/2 teaspoons of the salt and leave for 20 minutes to extract the moisture. Meanwhile, soak the dried mushrooms in hot water, then rinse and chop. Rinse and drain the vegetables. Mix with the mushrooms and 1 1/2 tablespoons of the vinegar, stir well, drain and set aside.

Split the prawns in half from the back, but without shelling them. Thread on a skewer lengthways and simmer in salted water (the skewer is to prevent them rolling around while being cooked). Remove the prawns from the heat when they turn pink, and leave to cool in the pan. Shell the prawns and slice lengthways into 2 or 3 pieces.

Mix the beaten eggs with 1/2 teaspoon of the salt and 1 teaspoon of the sugar. Scramble in a dry frying pan, stirring constantly to prevent sticking. Remove from the heat and sieve while still hot, then leave to cool on a serving dish.

Combine the remaining vinegar, salt and sugar and pour over the eggs. Mix well and serve with the vegetables.

Top: Vegetables with Scrambled Eggs and Prawns
Bottom: Sweet Red Beans

GLOSSARY

CHINESE CUISINE

Agar-agar: Used to make jelly. A seaweed derivative that solidifies without being refrigerated. Sold in powdered form in chemists and Chinese supermarkets.

Bamboo shoots: The Chinese use the sprouting shoots of certain bamboo plants, mainly two species (*Bambusa vulgaris and Phyllostachys pubescens*). Bamboo shoots can be bought in cans or grilled, but fresh shoots are best. If canned, remove them from the can, place in a bowl of cold water and store in the refrigerator. Sold in Chinese supermarkets.

Cashew nuts: Small sweet nut, sometimes sold raw, but usually sold roasted and salted in health food shops.

Chinese dried mushrooms: Most of the recipes in this book include dried mushrooms - they have a very penetrating flavour. Before use, soak them in warm water for 15 - 20 minutes, drain and squeeze out the excess water. The stalks are not used.

Chinese hot pepper sauce: Made from chilli peppers, salt and vinegar. Very hot and widely available.

Chinese leaf: Chinese leaf, "Pe Tsai", is a white cabbage, sweeter than the European one, with an elongated oval core and tightly packed leaves. Ordinary cabbage can be used in its place - if so, reduce the quantity and increase the cooking time.

Chinese noodles: There are two types of noodles used in Chinese cookery, and both are quite different to European noodles. "Fen Ssu" noodles are made from green soya seeds, and "Yang Fen" noodles are made from seaweed and look gelatinous. Both are used in fried dishes. Soya noodles should be boiled before cooking (average quality noodles are simply soaked in hot water). Seaweed noodles should be soaked in warm water for ten minutes before cooking. Both must not be overcooked, or they will go mushy.

Coriander: Leafy plant (*Corandrum sativum*) used in Chinese cuisine and an integral ingredient in curries. The Chinese name is "Yuen sai", and it is sold in most greengrocers.

Cucumber: Oriental cucumbers are about a third of the size of Western ones and are never peeled.

Five spice powder: Five spice powder is used frequently in Chinese cookery. It is reddish brown and is composed of star anise, fennel, cinnamon, cloves and a Chinese powdered root called "Sseu tch'ouan" (*Xanthoxylum pipesitum*). Five spice ("Hung liu" in Chinese) can be found in chinese supermarkets

Ginger: Very strong-tasting root of the ginger plant (*Zingiber officinale*). Normally used fresh, since the powder has a different taste. To store fresh ginger for a long time, chop the peeled root into chunks, cover with dry sherry and store in a covered container in the refrigerator.

Ginger is sold in most good greengrocers. "Red ginger" is ginger that has been conserved in red vinegar. The Chinese name is "Jeung".

Hoi sin sauce: Thick sweet reddish brown sauce, made from soya beans and chilli pepper. Can be substituted with black bean sauce or hot black bean sauce, this is a mixture of soya beans and chilli peppers.

Lotus buds: Large dried golden flowers with a very delicate taste. Said to be very nutritious. Soak in hot water for at least half an hour and cut in half for easy consumption. The cantonese name is "Khim chiam".

Lotus root (*Nelubium nuciferum*):Can be used fresh or dried. Peel the fresh root, slice into rounds, and use as indicated in the recipe. The dried root should be soaked for half an hour in hot water with a little lemon juice to prevent the lotus hardening. Can be stored for several days in a refrigerator. Preserved lotus root is sold in Chinese supermarkets.

Monosodium glutamate: Chinese name "Wei Ching", this is a vegetable salt extracted from seeds, particularly soya. It looks like coarse grained salt and has no taste of its own, but acts on the taste buds to enhance flavours. When food is well seasoned, it is superfluous, but some cooks add it automatically.

Red food colouring: Bright red food colouring powder is sold in Chinese supermarkets. It is used in small quantities to give the characteristic red colour of "lacquered/varnished" dishes.

Sesame seed oil: Mainly used in Chinese cookery to give flavour to vegetables.

Soy sauce: This is an indispensable ingredient in Asian cuisine, and comes in various grades of quality. The Chinese use both light and dark soy sauce. The first is used to season chicken, fish and delicately flavoured soups. Both types of sauce will keep indefinitely in the refrigerator.

Spring rolls: The thin sheets of pastry used to prepare the rolls can be bought in frozen packets from Chinese supermakrets. Defrost the pastry before unpeeling the sheets, and refreeze the unused sheets. No other pastry should be used to make spring rolls.

Star anise: Dried starshaped fruit from a tree native to China. Each fruit is made up of five petals that form a star shape; the Chinese name is "Pao Chiao" and it is widely used in Chinese cuisine, particularly for flavouring meat and poultry.

Tofu: Fresh tofu, made from soya beans is sold in Chinese supermarkets. Can be stored in water in the refrigerator, if the water is changed every day. Tofu has a consistency similar to blancmange, and is also sold in an easily reconstituted powdered form. The Chinese name is "Dow foo".

Water chestnuts: Water Chestnuts (*Eleocharis tuberosa*) are canned and exported to Europe via Hong Kong. Finely sliced, they are used in

many Chinese dishes, and can be bought in cans from Chinese supermarkets. Once opened, they will keep in the refrigerator for 7-10 days, if the water is changed every day.

Wok: This is the most basic untensil in Chinese cookery, since it can be used for boiling, braising, frying and steaming. Anything that can be done in western saucepans and frying pans can be done with a wok. It has a semispherical shape, which allows the food to be stirred easily without spilling over, and the metal sides are very thin so the high temperatures needed for fast Chinese coking can be reached quickly.

JAPANESE CUISINE

Ajino Moto: Brand of monosodium glutamate widely used in Japan.

Bream: A river fish also found in lakes, highly esteemed by the Japanese.

Dashi: Soup made from dried pieces of striped tunny and seaweed. The ingredients of this soup, powdered dried tunny (katsoubushi) and seaweed (kombu) can be found in specialised shops. See recipe on page 49.

Gingko nuts: From a tree native to Japan and China (*Gingko biloba*), these nuts have a distinctive taste and are eaten toasted like walnuts. They are added to many dishes to give flavour. Usually sold in cans.

Gohan: This is the Japanese name for cooked white rice.

Katsoubushi: Shredded dried tunny, used to make Dashi.

Kombu: Japanese dried seaweed in the form of wide dark grey strips. Used to flavour various dishes Can be stored indefinitely. Also sold preserved in vinegar.

Mirin: Japanese rice wine, sweeter than sake, and only used in cooking. Can be substituted with dry sherry.

Poppy seeds:(*Papaver somniferum*) are frequently used in various oriental cuisines to thicken curry sauces.

Rice bran: Obtained when rice grains are husked.

Sake: Japanese rice wine, usually served hot - just heat the jug of sake in hot water for a few moments. Widely used in Japanese cuisine, and can be substituted with brandy or dry sherry.

Shiritaki: Chewy transparent noodles, used in Japan for various dishes.

Shiso: The aromatic leaves of a perennial plant that is only used for culinary purposes by the Japanese and Vietnamese. The two varieties, red and green, are used to season pickles, and the seeds are used to make "sashimi".

Shungiku: Green leafy vegetable of the chrysanthemum family very popular in Japan. Can be substituted with cooked spinach, thistles or mustard leaves.

INDEX